Praise for *Simp*

"Curt Remington has written an inspiring book that goes far beyond the joyous benefits of meditation alone. Simple Meditation: A Spiritual Connection for Transforming Your Life will assist you in experiencing the direct divine connection that is your birthright—right here, right now—within your everyday reality. The insights offered in this beautiful and transformative book will propel you onward and upward on your path!" ~**Annie Burnside, author of** *Soul to Soul Parenting*

"Curt, your nature photography is absolutely stunning and your meditations simply wonderful. How lovely that you have combined all of this beauty with your personal journey and translated it into book form to help others. You are a gift to the world. I cannot wait for your new book to come out. Wishing you and your readers so much love, peace, joy, beauty and Spirit all around. Namaste." ~**Lori Boatman, author of** *Reannce and the Fifth Dimension*

"Brilliant insights about blending the spiritual practices of life with heart, nature and the sciences. Provides matter of fact, simple steps to improve you health and happiness. Awesome!" ~**Joy Gilfelen, president of UnitingCreatives.com and producer of** *Flipping the Joy Switch* **dvd**

"You are an excellent writer, the best I've had all year. It was a great pleasure to work on your manuscript." ~**Arlene Prunkl, PenUltimate Editorial Services**

"Through meditation, you can learn to think more clearly, work more efficiently and let go of stress. Whatever form your practice takes, let it be a part of your daily life. It is time well spent and the rewards are limitless." ~**Dawn Groves, author of** *Meditation for Busy People*

"As Curt describes in this book, a vision quest trip can be a life-changing experience." ~**Darcy Ottey, executive director of Rite of Passage Journeys**

Praise for Curt's website and articles

"Your website is so amazing, so inspiring! I love the texts, and I love the photos. There's such a beauty and harmony. Thank you for that place for meditation and for your friendship!" ~**Cirka Cernering**

"Beautiful. I loved reading this...brought tears to my eyes. I do a walkabout on a smaller scale quite often in the woods or in my kayak on a quiet body of water and sometimes in my garden as I create a little more beauty in my environment. Can't wait to read your book! ~**Linda Lee**

"I am bowled over. You put things in such a simple straightforward way — one of the hardest things for most of us who try to write. This is amazing and so sweet and well done. You are a good story teller. I'm so excited for you! And your Meditation Resources — what a gift!" ~**Amy Schwantes**

Simple
Meditation

Simple
Meditation
A Spiritual Connection For
Transforming Your Life

Curt Remington

Meditation Resources
Bellingham, Washington

Simple Meditation: A Spiritual Connection for Transforming Your Life

For more resources and information, visit www.meditationresources.net and www.curtremington.com.

First Edition

Cover and interior design by Curt Remington
Photography, including cover, by Curt Remington
Edited by Arlene Prunkl

ISBN: 978-1-936610-06-8
LCCN: 2010918430
Library of Congress subject headings:
meditation
spiritualism

Published by
Meditation Resources, Inc.
34 Longshore Ln
Bellingham, WA 98229, USA

Printed in the United States of America

To my dear wife, Mary, and to Chief,
for all their help and support
throughout this project.

Table of Contents

INTRODUCTION

Have you ever felt as if there should be more to life? A deeper meaning or greater purpose? Less stress? More happiness? Maybe more of a spiritual connection?

I'll bet you've even had moments when you experienced this spiritual connection, times when you were fully involved in what you were doing, blissfully happy and thinking of nothing else. Maybe you were sitting on a beach listening to waves roll into shore. Or you may have been in the mountains, gazing in awe at a spectacular view. Maybe you were looking into a crib, watching your baby sleep.

Wherever you were, it was a moment when your thoughts got out of the way, so you could experience that deeper, inner part of you, the spiritual part that is naturally calmer, wiser, and happier, the part that understands all things are connected.

In the pages of this book, you'll find the information and tools you need to experience more of that spiritual part of you, the part that can let thoughts go and be fully in the present.

Tuning into the details of nature is a wonderful way to let go of other thoughts and to start meditating. You could sit calmly in the woods, listening to the birds sing or the wind blow through the trees. Spending this time in nature puts you in a healthy environment, connected to the energy of a beautiful place.

Such escapes to nature kept me sane during the 1990s, while I worked seventy-hour weeks running a real estate appraisal business. Eventually, I started to learn and develop meditation techniques that went even further than connecting with nature, and I could do them without leaving the comfort of home.

Although we spend our days rooted in the physical world that we can see, we are part of a vast field of quantum energy that we can't see. The chapter on spiritual connections provides insight into those unseen, heavenly aspects of our universe that affect our lives every day. By understanding and working with the spiritual realm, we can improve the quality of our lives on earth.

Many of the exercises in the following chapters use the power of visualization to tap into this unseen energy, using it to access information or to release blocks to your emotional, physical, and spiritual well-being. One of the easiest ways to release these blocks is through an exercise that runs more energy through your system, keeping it clean like a mountain stream.

Relationships are a key factor in the quality of our lives. Meditation can help you let go of anger, resentment, and fear, blocks to great relationships. Not only will this improve your relationships, but improving those relationships will make it much easier to meditate.

Chapter 9, on walkabouts and vision quests, suggests a trip into nature to tie this all together. Your trip doesn't have to be a rugged wilderness outing. It could simply be a weekend dedicated to following some simple steps to connect with nature, meditate, review your life, and use the tools you'll learn in this book to examine your life's purpose. It can be a powerful and life-changing experience.

Throughout this book, I will also share some of my own experiences in my quest to find my purpose in life. I have not always been an avid meditator, at least not officially. Much of what held me back was a set of preconceived notions about meditation—what it is and what it isn't. If I'd understood the vast variety of techniques, the benefits, and the bliss of meditating, I would have started much sooner.

The exercises in this book are so simple and effective that you will start seeing results quickly, even if you've avoided formal meditation until now. Don't wait any longer. As you read this book, take the time to try the meditation exercises that you'll find throughout the chapters.

Welcome to an important next step on your spiritual journey.

CHAPTER 1
THE WHO, WHAT, WHERE, WHEN, WHY, AND HOW

What It Is and How to Do It

Be assured that you do not have to sit still and keep your mind blank. That isn't even possible—at least it wasn't for me. Meditation involves a calm aware‐ness with a focus on something that slows the usual stream of thoughts racing through your head. That sounds a lot easier, doesn't it? Once you slow that stream of thoughts, your mind relaxes and reaches a deeper state of awareness. Your body responds by letting go of its tension and stress.

On what could you turn your focus to quiet your mind and slow your stream of thoughts? Many forms of meditation exist with different themes and points of focus. Breathing is a common one, used by Buddhists and thousands of others throughout the world. Others include chanting a mantra such as *Om*, awareness of body sensations, prayer, visualization exercises, and countless other techniques. In this book, you'll find some of these techniques, the ones that I believe will be most beneficial to you.

Among the exercises included here are powerful meditations that release blocks to your flow of energy. Releasing these blocks is an important function of acupuncture, yoga, reiki, tai chi, and other eastern practices. You'll also find exercises for tapping into the field of energy that surrounds us, allowing you to access your psychic abilities.

Very Simple Meditation Exercise

To get started meditating, let's walk through a very simple and relatively easy exercise. This will give you a taste for what meditation is, if it's new to you. Like any meditation, it will get even easier with practice.

To try this exercise, find a quiet room where you will not be disturbed for fifteen minutes. You may sit on the floor, with your legs crossed pretzel-like in a full lotus position, with your feet on opposite thighs. I prefer a comfortable recliner or chair, with my feet on the floor. This better fits the simple meditation description. Your blood and energy can then flow freely. If you're used to or are more comfortable in another position, then by all means use it.

Once you're comfortably situated in your quiet place, inhale deeply, drawing air all the way down to your abdomen. As you exhale, release any tension.

Take a few more deep breaths, and relax your muscles. As thoughts come pouring through your head, observe them, and then let them go, without analyzing or adding to them. Let the simple noting of your thoughts, and letting them go, be your focal point. Like a kayak drifting in a river, let your consciousness float in the river of thoughts, without focusing on any one of them. If your thoughts don't seem to be enough of a focal point, try imagining that you're in a kayak, drifting and turning with the flow of your thoughts.

If you get distracted, observe this, then let it go and return to your gentle drifting. With practice, it will get easier and eventually the waves of thoughts will get calmer. Continue like this for your allotted time, or as long as you want. When you're done, take a few more deep breaths and come back to this book, or relax and take a break.

That was pretty simple, wasn't it? I chose this exercise first because many non-meditators seem to believe, "Meditation doesn't work for me. I can't stop thinking, so I can't possibly meditate." This exercise demonstrates that you don't have to stop your thoughts, you just have to be willing to let them go, rather than letting them take over. Even experienced meditators still have thoughts—thank goodness. They're just more experienced at letting them go and getting back to their meditation.

Why Meditate?

A great number of studies have been done on the benefits of meditation, published by Yale University, Harvard University Medical School, and many oth-

ers. The studies show that meditation:
- Reduces stress, anger, anxiety, and tension
- Improves concentration and attention
- Enhances energy
- Lowers blood pressure and helps heart disease
- Builds self confidence
- Helps cure insomnia
- Helps cure addictions
- Helps control weight
- Decreases muscle tension and related pain
- Reduces pre-menstrual symptoms
- Enhances the immune system
- Improves relationships
- Strengthens spiritual connection
- Helps in finding answers to life's difficult questions, and easy ones too
- Ensures that you will live happily ever after

Okay, I made the last one up. But it does make it more likely that you'll live happily, and you'll become more aware of the part of you that lives ever after. There are more benefits than I can possibly think of or list here, certainly more than enough to make it worth your while. With all these benefits, you'd think everyone would be meditating.

When to Meditate

You can be flexible about when you meditate, as long as you do it regularly. Some great times to meditate are when you're already in a serene state of mind, or conversely, when stress is building and you really could stand to let go of some. As you arrive home from work, you can use it to shift into a relaxed mode.

For many people, morning is the best time. You may be more alert in the morning, when the house tends to be quieter, at least if you can manage to get up before the rest of the household or wait until they leave. I have a hard time getting up before everyone else, and I work at home, so afternoons work well for me. Other people prefer to meditate right before bed, so they can get a good night's sleep. Anytime you feel like it is a good time to meditate.

To get the most benefit, try to set aside twenty minutes a day. You may start with just ten or fifteen and work up to twenty. The most important thing is to make it a regular habit. Missing an occasional day or cutting a session short won't hurt, and if you miss a few days, forgive yourself and start up regularly again. By doing it every day, you'll start seeing the benefits, and it will become a ritual you'll relish. Most of us have hectic lives, which is why it's important to meditate regularly. It forces us to take time for ourselves, to relax and unwind. Often, when we're busiest is the time we need meditation the most.

Where to Meditate

We've already discussed meditating in a recliner in a quiet room. While this is convenient, warm and dry, there are advantages to sometimes meditating in other locations.

For one thing, you're not always in a quiet room, yet it's almost always good to meditate. Some obvious exceptions are while driving and operating heavy machinery. Perhaps you work in an office cubicle, surrounded by noise and are feeling a great deal of stress. Reaching a calm, meditative state might be just what you need. If you have trouble sleeping, meditating while lying in bed can help you let go of stressful thoughts that are keeping you up in the middle of the night.

Meditating can bring a strong sense of connection with your surroundings. If you're going to be one with your environment, it's ideal to meditate in a beautiful, peaceful place. For this reason, I delight in meditating at parks, beaches, in the mountains, or kayaking down a river. A quiet corner of your yard might also be a good choice.

Who Should Meditate

You! Indeed, everyone would benefit from meditating. By the time you finish reading this book, I think you'll be plenty convinced.

For most of my life, I hadn't tried *formal* meditation. Like many people, I had the preconceived notion that meditating requires sitting still and "blanking" your mind. Not only did that sound impossible, but it sounded like a terrible waste of time.

In fact, meditating had been an important priority for me, but I hadn't realized that's what I was doing. I craved moments like lingering in the woods, taking in the solitude of my surroundings, or sitting on a beach and listening to waves lapping at the shoreline.

These were moments when I felt truly calm and at peace. I wasn't thinking about the past or the future. I was just content to be in the here and now. The most intense moments occurred while standing at the top of a mountain, looking out in awe of the splendor before me. I'd feel a part of something bigger, as if I knew with certainty what had meaning and what didn't.

Maybe that spiritual part of me did know. The less deep "ego" part of me reached a much simpler conclusion: that my destiny must be to live in the mountains, or at least to spend as much time there as I could. However, that would be difficult since I lived in Minnesota.

For years, I found a temporary fix that gave me such moments—whitewater kayaking. At the peak of my whitewater obsession, I wasn't sure why I felt such a strong desire to kayak every chance I got. Each weekend, I would call my friends, load up my gear and drive a few hours north to rivers such as the Kettle, the St. Louis or the St. Croix.

With the kayak at the river's edge, I'd struggle into my drytop and spray skirt, then squeeze into a compact whitewater kayak. The dull roar of the rapids and misty spray added to the anticipation, as I pushed off into the river. Maneuvering through boulders and waves, I would paddle toward my goal, the first medium-sized surfing wave with a calm eddy alongside it. I'd crash through the wave and make my way into position in the eddy, behind a line of kayakers wearing bright-colored helmets and waterproof jackets.

After a few minutes, my turn on the wave would come. I'd paddle like crazy, facing upstream, to get from the eddy onto the face of the wave. The current tried to spin my kayak and push me off the wave, but a quick stroke would straighten the kayak and keep me on course. Once on the face of the wave, gravity did its thing. The kayak would skim over the water, held in place by the wave as water rushed underneath. My arms knew what to do: they'd rudder the kayak to keep it pointed upstream. I wouldn't really be going anywhere, but it didn't matter. Right then, I was completely in the moment. I felt the surging wave and sensed the beautiful forest around me. They were just there, like me, and maybe a part of me. Somehow, I felt connected to all of it, *and it felt marvelous!*

I wasn't thinking about work, next week, or even tomorrow. Rather than a thought, there was more of a spiritual sense that heaven was right there, and I was somehow a part of it. That sense renewed my real love for life.

After taking turns surfing more waves, we'd set off downstream. In a serene section of the river, I would drift, eyes closed and head turned up, relishing the warmth of the sun. Again, a sense of serenity would come over me, along with a great feeling of connection to the river, the rocky shoreline, and the surrounding woods. I'd drift like that for a minute, turning with the current and listening to the birds, until my friends yelled, "Curt! Wake up and paddle. We've still got a mile to the takeout."

At the end of the day, and for the next few days, I would be more calm, happy, and content. I scarcely even wondered why. I only knew that I couldn't wait to kayak again the next weekend, so I'd spend much of the week reliving my last kayak adventure or dreaming of the one I planned for next weekend. It was a complete escape from my normal state of being, which was always on the run, with more work than I could handle and constantly scrambling to catch up. The kayaking helped me stay sane by giving me long moments of being fully alive in the present.

Intentional meditation didn't occur to me until I stumbled into it. Looking for answers to important questions, I visited Jill Miller, a wonderful psychic and teacher. I was so impressed with her reading that I signed up for a clairvoyance class. Much of the class focused on learning different forms of meditation. It didn't take long to realize that meditation has a variety of benefits, only one of which is increasing psychic ability. Kayaking and other outdoor pursuits were still great, but I found that I could reach a calm, focused state and be in the moment without loading up the gear and driving for hours. I also found that through meditation I became even happier, calmer, and more caring of my fellow man. I spent more of my daily life enjoying the moment, instead of always thinking about the past or the future.

In just a few years, I learned a great deal about meditation. It became clear that some of my favorite outdoor pastimes were actually simple but effective forms of meditation that I'll elaborate more on in this book. My clairvoyant training covered countless techniques, as we learned different meditations for a variety of purposes, like releasing the energy of traumatic experiences in our lives. I started experimenting with more methods, studying books, CDs, and videos. Eventually, many of my favorite exercises came to me psychically, after asking for a meditation for a specific purpose.

While meditating regularly, I began looking within for answers to important questions such as "what is my life's purpose?" I won't go too deeply into that right now, other than to say I believe an important part of that purpose is for me to share what I've learned along my path with you. I hope that you will find the information here helpful, maybe even life-changing. It certainly changed my life.

We tend to think of meditation in only one way.
But life itself is a meditation.
~Raul Julia (1940-1994), actor.

CHAPTER 2
CONNECTING WITH NATURE

In nature, everything works in cycles and tends to stay in balance. There is a strong interconnection between plants, animals, and the topography. Experiencing this rejuvenates your spirit and helps strengthen your bond with all that you're connected to, including the physical world around you, important people in your life, and the spiritual world that is silently guiding and supporting you.

Unfortunately, many of us have lost much of our connection with the earth. We live in big, insulated homes with controlled environments. We spend our day working with computers or other electronic devices, and then we come home and "relax" in front of a television, our computers, or more electronic devices. When we're focused on our computer screen or the television images, we experience a shrinking of our world.

In nature, we're more observant of and connected to our surroundings in an expansive way. Our senses open up to the damp smell of the forest, the cool breeze on our skin, the layer of pine needles beneath our feet, and the orange and pink clouds of the sunset. Spending time in the outdoors connects us with our more primal self, the one that understands without analyzing. By making this connection, we can return to our usual environment more aware and at peace.

Throughout the world's history, people lived in much closer contact with the earth than we do today. These people included farmers, fishermen, early settlers, and primitive tribes from Africa, Australia, ancient Europe, North America, and everywhere in between. North American Indians are a clear example. Each tribe had its own spiritual beliefs, but they almost all believed in the importance of the living earth. Closely working with nature, people hunted and grew their food and made clothing, shelters, weapons, and tools.

Relying more directly on the earth for their survival, Native Indians had to be highly attuned to their surroundings, alert for changes in the weather, the seasons, and animal habits, and aware of any dangers in their environment. Most also had a great love and respect for the land. They believed that the earth and its features had a spirit of their own and that all things are connected. Being connected didn't just apply to nature either. There was also a strong sense of connection to one another, as people lived and worked together to gather food, set up camps, and raise children. Spirituality was an important part of day-to-day life.

Some wise Native Americans spoke of this connectedness. Black Elk, an Oglala Sioux medicine man, said, "The first peace, which is the most important, is that which comes from within the souls of men when they realize their relationship, their oneness, with the universe and all its powers and when they realize that at the center of the universe dwells the Sacred, and that this center is really everywhere, it is within each of us."

Big Thunder, an Algonquin, said, "The Great Spirit is in all things, he is in the air we breathe. The Great Spirit is our Father, but the earth is our Mother. She nourishes us, that which we put into the ground she returns to us..."

Chief Seattle said, "Things are connected. Whatever befalls the earth befalls the sons and daughters of the earth. Man did not weave the web of life. He is merely a strand in it. Whatever he does to the web, he does to himself."

This is not just a Native American concept. A quote from the Bible addresses connectedness. "For in fact the kingdom of God is within you. There is one God and Father of all, who is above all, and through all, and in you all."

This connection or oneness is also a key concept in Taoism, Hinduism, and Buddhism. Most importantly, it is a significant concept in Heaven or the Spirit World, one that my wise Sioux spirit guide said I should emphasize in this book. It's a good thing that he did, because in my current human state, I sometimes forget such things.

Modern quantum physics supports and describes this connectedness. Scientists have concluded that everything is actually made from energy, which I'll detail more in the next chapter. For now, it's enough to know that as energy, the earth has an aura, or an energy field around it, a spirit in a sense. Although most of us aren't aware of it, energy fills the seemingly empty space around us. Compare this to a tropical fish in the ocean that may sense there is empty space between it and the next fish. We know water fills that space, and that it can transfer heat, currents, sound, and light. We think of what is between us and the next person as empty space, but not only is there air, there is lots of energy.

This energy/matter that we don't see is part of an enormous energy field that also contains the earth and its mountains, oceans, trees, atmosphere, and all living creatures. It extends into space connecting planets, stars, galaxies, and everything else. Wow! That's a lot. This field has been called the Quantum Ocean, the Mind of God, the Source, and many other things.

Native American in a Forest

Now that we know everything is connected, let's get back down to earth and connect with nature as a way to meditate. When you connect with nature, you're sensing your connection to the Source, to everything else.

Spending time in a forest or meadow, keenly aware of your environment, can be a compelling form of meditation and can give you a new perspective on things, really capturing the moment. You may become caught up in the scene's grand beauty or keenly aware of the details of a tree, a flower, or a bug. Perhaps you will listen and watch as birds call to one another or as a rabbit forages for food.

To understand what I'm talking about, imagine the year is 1600 and you're a Huron Indian hunting for food. You wait calmly, sitting on a comfortable log, at the edge of an aspen grove. Young trees conceal you as you sit motionless, waiting for a deer to saunter down the trail in front of you. It's a crisp fall day, with the sun warming your skin and the woods around you. A slight breeze rustles the leaves and brings a fresh wooded scent.

As you wait, your eyes survey the woods, watching for any movement. Your ears are tuned to catch any unusual sounds. Your body remains motionless to avoid betraying your presence. If you find yourself thinking about tomorrow's chores, you gently remind yourself to tune back into your surroundings, letting go of all other thoughts and distractions. Almost as part of the woods, you feel calm and at peace, while still alert for any movement in the woods.

Then, you hear the crunch of a leaf to your left. Reluctant to turn your head and draw attention, you wait, hearing several more crunching noises. As the sound gets closer, you become excited and lose your meditative state, anxiously expecting a deer. Instead, you spot the darting movement of a gray squirrel looking for food. It's not the deer you waited for, but you realize the value has been the benefits you experienced from calmly waiting, observing, at one with your surroundings.

Hunting and Fishing

Our ancestors gathered food through hunting and fishing, activities that put them in direct contact with nature. Nature is still out there in all its vast glory, waiting for you to embrace it. Casting a bass lure near a grassy shore, again and again, can be a very soothing meditation, as it requires just enough focus to hold your attention. It also requires you to pay close attention to your environment, like that overhanging tree that could snag your lure.

And, of course, there is fly-fishing. Norman Maclean, in *A River Runs Through It* [University of Chicago Press, 1976], does a beautiful job of describing a meditative state. "I sat there and forgot and forgot, until what remained was the river that went by and I who watched. On the river the heat mirages danced with each other and then they danced through each other and then they joined hands and danced around each other. Eventually, the watcher joined the river, and there was only one of us. I believe it was the river."

Very much like the Huron Indian, modern deer hunters spend hours in a tree stand, calmly waiting, keenly aware of their surroundings. For many, hunting is an important source of leaner, healthier meat and a chance to experience firsthand what their ancestors might have as part of nature's food chain. You might also consider hunting the way that I do, stalking your game with a camera.

Gardening

Growing your own produce also connects you with nature's cycles and with your ancestral roots. Fresh, organic fruits and vegetables taste better and are healthier too. As you learn what helps the plants to grow larger and healthier, you learn more of how Mother Nature works.

Tending a yard or a strictly aesthetic garden can also be a great source of joy and beauty, not only for yourself but for anyone who passes by.

Hiking, Skiing, and Climbing

Other sports such as hiking, climbing, and skiing can also be a form of meditation. The rhythmic repetitive motion of these sports can be a focal point in itself, allowing you to tune into what you're doing while you let go of other thoughts. These activities can also carry you far into the wilds and help you reach scenic, secluded places for meditating, with another focal point being the beauty that surrounds you.

Natural Focal Points

There are many ways to commune with nature, and you can begin by simply sitting down and tuning into your environment. You don't have to get out of the city, if that's where you live. Parks, ponds, and small havens for wildlife can be found in urban areas. Pay close attention to your surroundings and you'll find many things to focus on that will slow that stream of thoughts racing through your mind and better connect you with the energy of your environment.

• A beautiful scene—mountains and beaches are

wonderful, but it could be a waving wheat field
- Water sounds, such as a gurgling creek, rain, or waves lapping at a boat or shore
- The sound of wind through the trees
- The dancing flames of a fire
- Bird sounds and activity—consider placing a feeder or bath outside your window
- Other wildlife such as squirrels, deer, or insects—consider a trip to the zoo for variety
- A rising or setting sun and its gradually changing lighting
- Clouds as they move across the sky in ever-changing shapes
- If you're indoors, try meditating on a beautiful CD of nature sounds

If you live in the middle of a large city, you may even find manmade focal points that work well for you, such as the hum of machinery, the view over a cityscape, or the sounds of a busy park and laughing children. Unfortunately, some city noises aren't as soothing as the sounds you would find in a remote wilderness. If you find the sounds distracting, take note of them, then let them go and tune into something else, such as bumblebees pollinating flowers.

Tune into Nature Meditation

Reading about nature meditation is a good start, but now it's time to put it into practice. Find a nearby park, garden, pond, forest, or backyard, and make your way to a comfortable place to sit. For your first time, finding a quiet place without lots of people passing by would be a good idea. Meditating is easier without distractions. If you can't find time now, feel free to mark this page and come back to this exercise later.

On the way to your comfortable spot, pay close attention to your surroundings. Take note of unusual sounds or smells. What is the light like? Do you feel warm or cold? Do you notice any breeze? Are there interesting people or animals around you?

Once you've reached your destination, sit down and relax. What is there for you to tune into? Is there a beautiful scene? Whatever it is, take note of it, and use it as a focal point for your meditation. If it's a sound, you can close your eyes. Take a few deep breaths and tune into whatever you chose. If you find that you're thinking about the past or the future, remember to come back to your original focus, and stay in the moment. Sense your connection to all that is around you: the ground, trees, air, animals, and any people too. Feel this connection, sense it, without giving it much thought. Do this for as long as seems comfortable. When you're done, take a few deep breaths and stretch.

On your way home, try to retain your calm state and stay alert to your surroundings, watching for whatever might catch your attention. It's a magnificent world we live in, but much of the time we are too busy to notice.

Nature Photography

If you venture out with a camera in hand, you are likely to notice more. In other words, your time in nature can become a more *focused* experience. You may notice a well-balanced composition, the color of the clouds, or a fascinating pattern of rocks in a stream, things that could make a great picture. You may even decide to hunt wildlife with a camera, moving quietly through the woods, watching closely for birds, deer, or other potential photo subjects. Nature photography helps teach you to wait patiently for wildlife to move into position, to wait for ideal lighting or for an exquisite composition. All of these help keep you in the present moment. Along with learning mindful skills that teach you to be calm and focused, you can come home with beautiful images too.

Nature Photo Visualization Meditation

When the weather isn't cooperating or you don't have the time to go out into nature, you can use a beautiful picture to help you meditate and tune into the energy of a place. The technique is similar to the Tune into Nature Meditation, except you can do this in a comfortable chair at home. This is a good first step into visualization meditations, which can be powerful and fun. Practicing this exercise and improving your visualization skills will improve the power of other visualizations we'll use for healing or accessing psychic abilities.

For this exercise, choose a picture of a place that appeals to you. If you don't have such a picture at home, there are plenty on my website at curtreming-ton.com. Sit down and take a good look at the picture, visualizing the entire place, not just what you see in the photo. What details would you find in that place that you could tune into? If it's a beach scene, there might be waves lapping at the shore. Perhaps it's a forest setting, with wind rustling through the trees. Is there sun that would be warming and soothing?

When you're ready, close your eyes and imagine that you're there. Feel the energy of the place surrounding you. Visualize the scenery as clearly as you can. Try to add other senses to your visualization. Is the air cool or warm? What scents does it carry? Do you hear birds? A babbling creek?

Once you've created the scene in your mind, tune into a detail to focus on. For instance, if the picture is of a beach, imagine the constant sound waves would make as they roll into shore. If it's a wooded scene, what would the wind sound like, rustling the leaves? Focusing on such an aspect will allow you to let go of your other thoughts. Enjoy this beautiful place for as long as you like. Ten minutes is a good goal to start with. When you're ready, take a deep, clearing breath or two, open your eyes, and return to the comfort of your home.

As you practice visualizations, it will become easier to add more of your senses and more details, like a foreground, middle, and background. Adding movement can also intensify your images. Try changing angles or visualizing the rolling waves, swaying trees, or whatever might be moving in your scene.

Beaches and Deserts

Nature holds a variety of special places to visit or to visualize. Beautiful islands, beaches and bays can be very soothing. Since ancient times, people have flocked to beaches as a place to escape and relax. These places combine the warm sun's rays, the sand's connection to the earth, the soothing sound of the waves and the vast expanse of ocean, with its constantly changing surface and endless mysterious depths.

Like the ocean, deserts are vast and mysterious. They tend to be very peaceful with starlit skies that light up as if you are floating in space. While beaches are places where many people gather, in a desert you can find serious solitude. Some desert places such as Sedona, Arizona, parts of Egypt, and Australia have unique and powerful energy vortexes, part of the earth's aura, which can help your spirits soar.

Mountain Man

As a place to meditate, mountains have a special, powerful energy of their own. Native Americans, and cultures throughout the world, have considered them sacred. Greek and other ancient mythologies considered mountaintops the home of the gods. Climbing high, the air is so fresh and light that it can be hard to breathe, but what you do breathe seems to purify your lungs and body. Returning to lower elevations, you tend to feel stronger and refreshed, even if your legs ache. You can experience the inspiration and energy of a mountain without climbing it. Viewing one, even as a photograph or painting, can remind us that there are special places on earth that reach up to connect with heaven.

At age sixteen, a visit to such a magical place had an enormous impact on me. A friend and I set off on a road trip to see the Canadian Rocky Mountains. We backpacked up a remote valley. As we gradually climbed higher, I felt as if I was getting closer to my true home. We reached a hut situated between an alpine lake, mountains, and a cliff top with panoramic views. A beautiful rainbow formed over the mountains to the south, reminding us that God's presence was there.

Being that close to heaven changed me forever. I decided that my destiny must be in the mountains, and that I wanted to be a mountain man, even if that hadn't been a popular career since about 1860. Sixteen-year-olds aren't always practical.

Through the rest of high school, I saved money and made plans to spend my first year out of high school camped in the Montana Rockies, just south of Glacier National Park. I got to Montana in the fall and spent much of my time hiking and exploring, trying to decide where to set up camp for the winter.

One hike stands out in my memory. It was a cool afternoon, and I was south of Glacier Park and high in the mountains. Even on Highway 2, there was little traffic. Once I turned onto a back road to the trailhead, there were no more signs of human life. I parked the truck and started the steep hike up through evergreen forests. Claw marks along the trailside stood much higher than I could reach, reminding me that this was grizzly bear country. The thought that there were more bears than people nearby gave me a little apprehension, so I talked to myself, more loudly than usual.

After what seemed like many miles, the woods ended and a small mountain beckoned directly ahead, much closer than the end of the trail, which turned left and continued far into the wilderness. I started scrambling upward, deciding the small mountain was my destination. Before long, I was on a ridge near the top with steep drops on each side. The ridge became sharper, with drops so steep that an unroped traverse seemed foolish. I looked back at what I'd already crossed and realized that getting to this point had probably also been foolish. I suddenly felt very vulnerable, realizing it was late in the day and a lot stood between me and the safety of my truck. I would need to recross the ridge and make my way back along a steep, scree-covered descent, and miles of forest. And I might encounter those bears.

Taking a deep breath of mountain air, I looked around at views of mountain after mountain for as far as I could see. Although I was alone, I felt connected to the rugged wilderness that surrounded me, to the rock below me, and to the heavens above me. I felt exquisitely alive! And I felt a great desire to stay that way. After taking in this grandeur for a few minutes, I turned to make my way back down. I managed to live through the long hike back, reaching my truck just after dark.

As much as I loved the mountains, however, it soon became obvious that connecting with other people was important too. Within a month, I was back in Minnesota.

For years after that, dreams of moving to a mountain state lurked at the back of my mind, even if it meant working a job in civilization. At first, I put the mountains on hold while pursuing a college education. After graduating, I made a few trips to the mountains and learned that well-paying jobs are hard to find in beautiful places. The mountains would have to sit on hold a little longer, until I had some savings. I stumbled into a career appraising real estate, a profession that would have never crossed my mind during college. More years went by, and then my soul mate Mary finally showed up in my life. We married shortly after my thirtieth birthday.

Eventually, Mary got into the appraisal business too, and we started Remington Appraisals. We built a successful business, and we were initially excited to be making a good deal of money. The effort took most of our time and energy. We worked far too many hours a week and eventually felt caught in a hamster wheel. The years churned by, highlighted by occasional vacations, including some mountain trips, and raising three usually adorable girls. We did manage to camp and take advantage of the beautiful lakes and rivers in Minnesota, but I continued to dream that we'd move to the mountainous West someday. We both eventually felt as though we were on the wrong track, working far too much. With a strongly entrenched work ethic, we had trouble turning over more responsibility to our employees so we could enjoy life more.

Yearning for change, we sold our appraisal business and moved to Bellingham, Washington. Not only did that put us in the foothills of the North Cascades Mountains, but it was also at a gateway to the San Juan Islands. We established an appraisal business there but kept our client base manageable, spending more time enjoying life, hiking, skiing, camping, and taking in the beauty of our new area. After years of hard work, not only did I have the partner, children, and financial stability I had dreamed of, but finally, I also had the mountains.

Yet once I had all that, something still seemed to be missing. At some point, it occurred to me that there might be more to life than meeting my own needs. Surely, I was meant to contribute more to humankind than lots of property appraisals. It was time to find my bigger purpose in life, or at least to write something important that people would read and that might have an impact on their lives. This book seemed like a good place to start.

Final Thoughts

Not everyone shares my intense enthusiasm for mountains, or even for nature, but everyone can get a great deal of benefit from going outdoors and tuning into the amazing world we live in. We all have natural beauty around us, like a beautiful flower, fascinating clouds, or ducks in a nearby pond. Taking the time to appreciate these things will bring us that much closer to finding peace and happiness.

Adopt the pace of nature: her secret is patience.
~**Ralph Waldo Emerson, author,** *Nature.*

CHAPTER 3
SPIRITUAL CONNECTIONS

Science and Heaven

The meditations we've covered will help you connect with the world around you, which you can see, hear, smell, and feel. At the same time, there is even more that you are connecting with but that you may be largely unaware of. You can call it heaven, the source, another plane, the spiritual world, or something else. Whatever you call it, it is there. We were all part of that spiritual realm before we were born, but have since forgotten. Meditation can help you become conscious once again of that spiritual realm that we are all a part of.

Like many of us, I spent most of my life grounded in the physical world, analyzing everything and skeptical about anything I couldn't see or verify myself. When my father was first diagnosed with cancer, my family was invited to an energy healing conducted by my sister's Episcopal minister, who is also a gifted clairvoyant. During the healing, she moved around the circle of family members, placing hands on each person's shoulders and performing some individual healing. As she did this, she described what each person was feeling or what was going on in their lives, without having met them before. Her comments for my family members were very accurate.

I could feel the energy in the room, and I had grown up having occasional psychic experiences. Still, I questioned whether she had gotten this information from someone in the group. When she said she could see guardian angels in the room, I doubted her. I couldn't see any. When she got to healing me, she kindly described my doubt, suggesting that I just wasn't tuned in today. Maybe she could see it in my eyes. She wasn't reading my mind or talking to my angels or guides, was she? How could she, if I couldn't see them or talk to them? I now realize that it could have been a very moving and healing experience, if I'd been more open-minded.

Since that time, I have developed my own clairvoyance and become more aware of the spirit world. It's clear to me now that she was doing exactly what she said she was doing. Why did I doubt her? Because for me at that time and for many of us, it's hard to conceive there is a spiritual world (another dimension) that surrounds us, but that we can't see.

We base our perception of reality on what we experience with five of our senses. We grow up believing the world is just the solid matter that we can *see*, made of atoms and molecules, even though visible light is only a narrow band of the many types of energy around us.

Quantum physicists have discovered that solid matter (molecules and atoms) actually consists of much smaller particles (quarks, leptons, etc.), and that these particles are a form of energy. Not only is matter actually made of energy, but this energy/matter also fills all the empty space around us. According to the Fermilab's[1] website, [http://fnal.gov] astronomers have studied how galaxies spin and have calculated that "...ordinary matter containing atoms makes up only 4 percent of the energy-matter content of the universe."[2] The rest of it is made up of other forms of energy-matter that we still know little about.

Scientists know that this matter can behave in strange ways. Subatomic particles can be in more than one place at a time. They react to thought, acting like an energy wave most of the time, and like a particle when observed. In other words, the fact that someone is observing them causes a change in their structure. They seem to communicate instan-

---

1   Fermilab is a US national laboratory for particle and nuclear physics, part of the US Department of Energy. http://home.fnal.gov/~dhooper/darkmatter.html.

2   Fermilab website, press room archives. http://www.fnal.gov/pub/presspass/press_releases/cdmsdata.html.

taneously and are linked on some level beyond space and time. In our four-dimensional world, this makes no sense, but quantum physicists now believe there may be up to eleven dimensions, which are largely a mystery. Many people cling to a viewpoint based on old science, consisting of a world made of solid matter with lots of empty space in between.

This old perception doesn't cut it anymore. It can't explain quantum mechanics, the thousands of documented near-death and out-of-body experiences, miraculous healings, past-life regressions, telepathy, mediums, and countless other phenomena that people have experienced all over the world. These experiences are explained by a vast field of this mysterious energy that surrounds and connects us all. Heaven (the spirit world) is also made of this energy, on a higher vibrational frequency than our physical world. As I mentioned before, this field has been called the Quantum Ocean, the Source, or the Mind of God. Historically, there has been a huge gap between science and religion or spirituality, but as new discoveries are made, that gap may continue to close, as we conclude that God is indeed everywhere and everything. Since we too are part of this field, God truly is in each of us.

Energy versus Matter

When you look closely enough, you'll find there is not much difference between solid matter and this other energy-matter stuff. That's because it is all energy.

You may have had a science class that covered the basic structure of an atom, that tiny particle that all those "solid" things are made of. A nucleus consists of protons and neutrons, with electrons orbiting around the nucleus. Between the nucleus and the electrons is a lot of "empty" space. In studying electrons, scientists have found that they can behave like particles when observed and like energy waves when they aren't observed. In

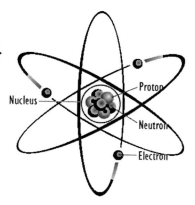

other words, they react to human thought. When that electron is in a particle state, it is part of what we call *solid matter*. In other words, not much is actually solid about "solid" matter.

Through clairvoyant and energy healing work, I've learned energy not only responds to thought but also is largely controllable by thought. When healers direct healing energy, it is through their thoughts that they tell the energy where to go and what to do.

This knowledge, that everything is made from energy and thought can control energy, can have an enormous impact on your life. Our positive thoughts can manifest positive results, as illustrated in many popular videos and books: *The Secret, The Law of Attraction, Seven Spiritual Laws of Success, Excuses Begone!, You Can Heal Your Life, What the Bleep Do We Know*. On earth, the effects of our thoughts are not always immediate, but can be very powerful and can shape our lives. Those people who constantly complain tend to get more to complain about. Those who expect their lives to go well usually find it to work out that way.

In the spirit world, where energy is less solid,

thought produces immediate and dramatic results. Spirits can do things such as create objects out of energy or change their appearance to whatever they wish. They can travel great distances with virtually no effort. Sounds like fun, doesn't it?

Although current science can't accurately describe heaven (the spirit world), other sources can and have described it very similarly, providing validation for one another. These include near-death experiences, spiritual regressions, and the work of psychics and mediums. My own experiences with out-of-body travel, communicating with spirits, and talking with other psychics confirm a spirit world very much as described in the books written by Dr. Michael Newton: *Journey of Souls, Destiny of Souls,* and *Life Between Lives: Hypnotherapy for Spiritual Regression.*[3] A psychologist and hypnotherapist, he discovered and refined a technique that enables people to remember their experiences in heaven before and between lives. Using this spiritual regression technique with over 7,000 clients, he has learned a great deal about heaven and our purpose here. Before he stumbled across this technique, much of what he learned was outside his own belief system.[4]

3　*Journey of Souls*, Llewellyn Publications: St. Paul, MN, 5th Revised Edition, 2003; *Destiny of Souls: New Case Studies of Life Between Lives,* Llewellyn Publications, 2001; *Life Between Lives: Hypnotherapy for Spiritual Regression, Llewellyn Publications, 2004.*

4　The Newton Institute for Life Between Lives Hypnotherapy. http://www.spiritualregression.org/.

My Introduction to the Spirit World

Along with the countless books that I've read, this information on the spirit world came from my own psychic readings, readings by my wife Mary, and other clairvoyants I know. During much of my career as an appraiser, I would have never imagined that someday I'd be doing psychic readings for strangers. Becoming open to such things was among the many changes, on my spiritual journey.

Once we moved west, we found more time to enjoy life. The mountains and islands provided many opportunities to revel in nature and slow our pace. Our life became more balanced. Still, as I mentioned earlier, something seemed to be missing. I felt that I needed to find *the meaning of life* or *my deeper purpose.*

During our first few years of exploring Washington and settling in, my father became increasingly sick with metastatic prostate cancer. He'd apparently avoided doctors for some time, so by the time it was discovered, all they could do was slow it down for a year or so. While he was ill, I traveled to Minnesota to visit, and he flew out to visit us a few times, enjoying the beautiful scenery in our area and participating vicariously in our adventures.

My father's health eventually took a turn for the worse, and he moved into an assisted-living facility. This was enough to get me thinking and reading about spirituality and my own mortality. I knew that my dad had avoided facing his mortality for as long as possible: putting off dealing with doctors, having to move out of his rural home, or talking about death. In my attempt to help him face his reality and overcome some of his fear of death, I sent him a copy of *Destiny of Souls* along with a greeting card. Part of the card mentioned, "You will soon be free of your uncooperative body, and I'm confident that you will be on to great adventures with new energy and enthusiasm." According to my sister, he was "delighted" with the package.

At the end, his condition rapidly worsened. I flew to Minnesota and arrived to find him heavily drugged and incoherent. My two sisters and I took turns staying with him. In the middle of the night, holding my sister's hand, he breathed his last breath. Back at my sister's house, where I was sleeping between shifts with Dad, I suddenly sat up in bed, awakened by a vivid dream of a galloping horse. A minute later, my sister called to let me know that dad had just stopped breathing. I realized that the galloping horse represented him, letting me know that he was free of his pain-ridden body and had moved on to new adventures. A mixture of emotions overcame me, especially relief and happiness for him, because he truly must be in a better place.

I'd had occasional psychic experiences for years, so I'd always been a believer in some sort of spiritual world. After my father's death, my psychic experiences and fascination with them grew stronger. I had more and more dreams about Dad and started reading books on spiritual and psychic subjects. When I sat down to contact my spirit guides, communication was spotty, but I'd occasionally see my father or other spirits. They seemed friendly, as if wanting to help, but I couldn't really understand them. Wanting to know more, I did an Internet search and found Jill Miller,[5] right here in Bellingham. She's been a psychic and spiritual teacher for over thirty years.

Jill's clairvoyant reading was remarkably accurate. She seemed to know what was going on in my life, and she communicated with my father. She also described a number of my spirit guides and the messages they had for me. I was so impressed by her reading that I signed up for her six-week class to develop my own psychic abilities. After that, I signed up for another year of classes and eventually graduated from her Advanced Clairvoyant Program. Jill generously shared much of what she's learned in her years of psychic reading and teaching.

One of the most important things I gained from my experience was a shift in thinking, viewing myself as an eternal soul with a temporary body, rather than as a body who happens to have a soul. I also learned that we reincarnate many times to learn lessons on earth. Between lives, we return to heaven, where we spend time sharing, examining what we learned, and recovering from the trials of life here. We also work on choosing and preparing for our next life. We eventually learn all we need to learn on earth and quit reincarnating, devoting all of our time to the spirit world.

Much of Dr. Michael Newton's work has been to study our "life between lives", which is also the title of his most recent book. Psychiatrist and healer Brian Weiss[6] has done similar work, focusing more on our

5   www.jillmillerpsychic.com.
6   www.brianweiss.com.

lives here on earth rather than our time between lives. He has used past-life regression to help many patients remember a past life in order to treat issues that continue to trouble them in this life.

Even while we are here, busy with this life, a part of us is aware of and in communication with heaven. This part of us is commonly referred to as our "higher self," "spiritual self," or "inner being." Our higher self is much wiser and more enlightened than our ego or conscious mind. This is an important concept that I'll cover in more depth later.

The deep relaxation exercise below is a good warm-up for any other meditation. Accessing past-life memories or psychic abilities is much easier in an alpha or theta brainwave state, in other words, a state of deep relaxation.

Relaxation Exercise

Find a comfortable chair and sit with your feet on the floor. Make sure your clothing is loose and comfortable and there are no distractions to interrupt you. Rest your arms on your lap or the arm of the chair. Close your eyes. Take a deep breath, exhale, and let your tension out along with your breath. Remember to breath in relaxed manner, as you continue the exercise, occasionally drawing in a few especially deep, cleansing breaths to release any tension.

Shift your awareness to the top of your head. Imagine a tingling sensation or flow of energy at the top of your head, followed by deep relaxation that flows down the back of your head to the base of your neck. As you imagine this, you will create it. Feel the relaxation work its way around to your face and throat. Take note of how relaxed your head now feels.

Next, shift your attention to your neck. Feel the same tingling or energy, followed by relaxation that works down your shoulders and arms. When it reaches your hands, squeeze and relax them, letting any tension flow out your palms.

Feel this tingling of energy in your back, which works down your spine until your entire back is relaxed. From there, feel it work around your torso and around into your abdomen and organs. Let them relax.

Feel this same sensation in your hips and groin. Let any tension move down your legs, as you feel your thighs relax and then your knees, continuing down your legs as any tension is released through the bottom of your feet.

Enjoy this deep state of relaxation until it's time to finish or you're ready to move on to another exercise.

Past-Life Meditation

Before doing this exercise, it would be helpful to warm up with the relaxation exercise or another meditation, such as the very simple meditation exercise, at the beginning of this book, or the tuning into nature in chapter 2. Once you learn the grounding and running your energies exercises, covered in later chapters, I'd suggest starting with those.

Once you're in a calm, clear meditative state with your eyes closed, gently hold the intention of tuning into a past life. You can even specify a time period or a particular type of life, like a life with someone you're close to or a life when you were rich, brave,

*poor, or whatever. With that intention, wait and see
what comes up. As an alternative to just "tuning in,"
you can visualize yourself walking down a hallway
with a number of doors, then choosing one, opening
the door, and stepping through. Once you've tuned in,
or stepped through the door, you may get a sense of
something. An example could be feeling great space
and desert air around you, or sensing the stone walls
of ancient buildings. Images may start taking shape,
like woods or teepees, possibly a snowy tundra. Relax
and try to explore. A good first step is to look down
at your shoes or bare feet. They may give you a good
clue as to the era. Can you see what else you're wearing? Is someone with you? Do you sense that you also
know them in this life? If all you're seeing is the back
of your eyelids, relax and enjoy your calm meditative
state. This may take practice.*

*If you are getting good pictures, try moving for-
ward in time and see what happens. To do this, you
only have to intend it. Did you marry? Did you have
children? Are there people from that life that are also
in this life? What lessons did you learn in that life? If
you feel up to it, you can even move to the end of that
life. There can be important messages in how your life
ended and in any life review you might have done.
Once you come out of your meditative state, more questions may arise, such as how the lessons in that life
may pertain to the life you're in now. Did you have
a trauma in that life that is causing you trouble in
this life? Were there unresolved lessons that you continue to work on now? Take the time to look at these,
and try this technique again later. The more that you
practice, the easier this exercise will get.*

Example

As part of my clairvoyant class, we looked for a life in which we held others as slaves. With that intention in mind, what came up for me was a very primitive life as a tribal leader in Europe, thousands of years ago. Our cave sat up on a hill, with a fire pit in front. We captured half a dozen men from another tribe and tried to force them to work. They resisted constantly, so we eventually gave up and let them go.

Spirit World

So, what is heaven like? It's a place of love and learning, where souls are working to advance in their spiritual enlightenment. Since the spirit world consists of energy on a higher vibrational frequency than here, spirits and their surroundings are less solid than our physical world. Much of what's been created in heaven bears a striking resemblance to life on earth, including beautiful parks, lakes, forests, mountains, and a variety of buildings, including pyramids, domes, crystal cathedrals, and a vast library building known as the Akashic Records. Many of the spirits in heaven had lives on earth, so it's natural that the spirit world would have earthlike features, or maybe it's that earth has heaven-like features.

Akashic Records

Among the fascinating things we did in clairvoyant class, was to take an occasional out-of-body trip to the Akashic Records. Wikipedia describes these records as "a compendium of mystical knowledge encoded in a non-physical plane of existence. [They] are described as containing all knowledge of human experience

and the history of the cosmos."[7] The records contain all knowledge of our earthly experiences, including some information on future events. Edgar Cayce[8], a famous psychic, obtained much of his information from the Akashic Records. For our class, Jill Miller would walk us through leaving our bodies behind. Our consciousnesses first traveled to the roof. From there, it took almost no time to reach a patio in front of an enormous library building with columns on either side of the entrance.

Once inside, we would each make our way to a desk and ask the librarian a question such as "Is there intelligent life on other planets?" (By the way, there is.) On the next trip, we might ask a personal

7   http://en.wikipedia.org/wiki/Akashic_records.
8   Edgar Cayce (1877-1945) performed thousands of psychic readings, with numerous books devoted to those readings. http://www.edgarcayce.org/are/edgar-cayce.aspx.

question such as "How many lives have I had?"

The information available at the Akashic Records is limitless; however, future events are less clear, due to the impact of individual free will. In other words, the choices we make can shape our future; it isn't written in stone. The librarians also withhold information that has the potential of doing harm. Trips to the Akashic Records are fascinating and much more fun than my school-days field trips to the local post office.

Transition to the Spirit World

At the end of our physical life on earth, we transition from one dimension to another, usually with the help of our angels and guides. We celebrate our homecoming with other spirits whom we've known since long before we were born, including loved ones who have already passed over and others we've known and will recognize once we get there. As part of a "soul group," we spend time in heaven, and in our lives on earth, with many of the same souls. In reviewing my own past lives, my wife, kids, and parents have appeared in many of them.

In heaven, there are classes and work specialties, like teaching or designing environments. Did you really think you just sat on clouds all the time? Young spirits focus on schooling, eventually moving into a career-like focus. A specialty for me, and one of my long-deceased childhood mentors, is working with soldiers killed in battle, helping them readjust after a sudden and often traumatic death. Another spirit with whom I've communicated works with very young spirits, doing a lot of supervision, much like a daycare provider. Energy healing is a popular specialty. One spirit with whom my wife recently spoke tutors students in how to create with energy.

In heaven, there is also fun and recreation such as art, dancing, music, and games. Spirits spend time reviewing what was learned in the last life and they look at options to prepare for their next life, then reincarnating until all their lessons on earth are mastered. After that, they continue to work on spiritual advancement on the next and higher planes. Many of these more advanced spirits decide to be teachers or spirit guides for those on earth who are still working on their life lessons.

Spirits can instantly change their appearance. I've seen them appear in a way most recognizable to their loved ones, just like the way they looked shortly before they died. They can also change to a younger, more favored look. They may choose an appearance that best gets their message across, such as wearing clothes from a memorable event or dressed for fly-fishing, to assure you that they're relaxed and enjoying themselves. Spirits can also appear as an aura of energy, without any earthlike shape.

Emotionally, souls leave this world shedding much of their hate, anger, and jealousy. In heaven, they experience more love, bliss, and a feeling of being more alive. That is not to say that they are perfect, once they leave this plane. I've encountered stuck spirits who still have some of the same problems they had on earth.

Alcoholics make a good example. They may still crave alcohol in the spirit world, but it's not available.

Such spirits look for a human who is drinking heavily, so they can move into their aura and experience the high. As the drinker becomes more intoxicated and starts losing control, the spirit moves in more to take over. Do you know someone who goes through a complete personality change when they're drinking? Once they're drinking, it may not be that person whom you're dealing with. No wonder the drinker doesn't remember what happened during their intoxication.

There are spirits at all levels of advancement, many of which never had a life on earth. Some have had lives on other planets or were already advanced before earth became habitable. Some are not yet ready for the rigors of life on a harsh planet like ours, or are on another spiritual path. During my clairvoyant classes, we encountered all sorts, ranging from simple spirits that you may find hanging around in a basement to archangels and ascended masters.

Scary Stuff

If you think this talk of spirits is scary stuff, let me assure you that you are not alone. The way that movies and television portray the spirit world would be enough to scare anyone. Throughout much of my life, I held some fear of the supernatural, especially of the occasional spirits I saw as a child. When I started clairvoyant training, my wife was very reluctant to join me, due to her fears. But once we each started developing our clairvoyance, the fears disappeared. Why? People naturally fear the unknown, and for us, the spirit world was no longer the unknown. Horror is the stuff of movies, most of the time, not reality.

Troublesome spirits don't have that much power here on earth, and we all have powerful spirit guides and angels protecting and watching over us. You can call on them anytime, using your thoughts to put out a request. We also have more of our own spiritual power than most of us realize.

Quite often, the spirits who scare people aren't even trying to cause trouble. They're just misunderstood. My wife and I did a reading for a young woman. She had sensed a spirit around her numerous times, making her scared of sleeping alone. Her fear also kept her from communicating with the spirit. We contacted that spirit. It was the woman's deceased mother, trying to convey love and a wish that she could still be there for her daughter.

One of my wife's first experiences turned out to be a similar misunderstanding. As I started developing my clairvoyance, Mary had no choice but to hear all about it almost constantly. She became more concerned about spirits in our house, especially in the middle of the night while we were asleep. One night she woke and saw a strange image of large, intertwined rings near the bedroom wall, which startled and mystified her. They seemed so surreal that later she questioned whether it had really happened. Later in a reading, we learned that her spirit guides were helping her to see a projection of her own spiritual energy. Their point was to help her realize that she is very clairvoyant too. They were probably anxious to get started on working with her.

After a year of her own clairvoyant training, Mary has encountered many spirits and isn't frightened by them anymore. Not only are they nothing like the horror films portray, but they also don't come from Hell. In fact, I'm quite sure there is no traditional Hell, with caves and flames. Criminal or bad behavior does have consequences though. The concept of karma does apply, so someone who's particularly bad in this life may be looking at a dose of their own treatment in the next. If a soul is especially cruel over a number of lives, they may face something more severe, like many years alone, on a desolate planet, to resolve their behavior. Spirits usually view this as a chance to examine and learn from their behavior rather than as a punishment. The worst that most souls will face is their own disappointment in any shortcomings when reviewing their life and feeling the effects they had on others, from the other person's point-of-view. Most spirits find the afterlife to be supportive and forgiving.

Loved Ones Are Still Around

After leaving the physical world, spirits still check on the loved ones they left behind. If you've ever dreamed of a loved one, or sensed their presence, it probably was them letting you know that they are there. They may even give you a sign to let you know they're okay. Before her father died, a friend of ours asked him to send a rainbow from the other side, to let her know he was okay. She now sees a lot more rainbows, not only outdoors but also as the sunlight passes through a window or light shines through an ornament. We psychically checked in with him about the rainbows, and he responded, "Yeah, I create them. Aren't they great?"

When you think of someone on the other side, it's like dialing their phone number. They can tune into your thoughts or hear what you are saying, so go ahead and tell them whatever it is you wanted to say but never got around to while they were alive. Even if you don't hear them respond, they hear you. They may also share in your joy during the highlights in your life, like a graduation, wedding, or even when you play the guitar and sing. When I reach a mountain peak and see a beautiful vista, I'll sometimes invite a few of my favorite spirits to come enjoy the beauty of that place. On one such occasion, I contacted Wolf, my totem animal/guide. My German shepherd suddenly got excited and started romping playfully in the snow. Apparently, he could see the fun-loving spirit guide.

This great awareness of the spirit world and our connection to it can enrich our lives here and give us a new perspective. Day-to-day issues that used to cause us stress become less important. Caring for each other and enjoying life become more important. We begin to feel more love toward one another knowing that we truly are all connected, learning here together. Death becomes less scary, knowing that our souls are infinite. Heaven is a loving place we call "home," where we reunite with old friends and family.

Spirit Guides and Guardian Angels

Throughout our lives and between lives, spirit guides and guardian angels are with us, teaching, caring, and helping in countless ways. When you feel you have a great intuitive hunch, it may actually be a message from a helpful spirit. They help you in ways that you wouldn't have thought of, like providing words of wisdom on important decisions or helping you heal an ailment or an issue.

For some time, I wasn't sure of the distinction between guardian angels and spirit guides, believing them to be different names for the same thing. I would occasionally see spirits that looked like angels, with wings and all. I figured that some spirit guides just preferred to look like angels. Eventually, it occurred to me to ask one of my spirit guides and an angel about this. What I got from them is that angels start out on a higher and slightly different spiritual level than spirits like us, that have human lives on earth. Most spirit guides have had lives on earth, however they don't become a spirit guide until they've reached a high level of advancement. Angels skip the whole earthly lessons in human bodies experience. Like spirit guides, they watch over and guide us. I've also been told that our guardian angels stay with us our entire life, whereas some spirit guides may be temporary, showing up when they're needed.

The archangels you may have heard of are real, very powerful, and ready to help. I've worked with Michael on issues around protection, solving problems and clearing energy. I've called on Raphael for help with healing physical ailments. Each archangel has their own specialty, which you can find on the Internet or in books about angels, such as those written by Doreen Virtue or Sonia Choquette. Archangels are capable of being in many places at once, so don't be concerned about taking them away from a duty of more importance. They will consider your request important too.

Ascended masters, or religious/spiritual leaders such as Jesus, Buddha, Lao Tzu, and Mohammed are also available to help and can be in many places at once. Wayne Dyer gives Lao Tzu credit for much of his most recent book.

What Do Spirit Guides Look Like?

A guide usually chooses an appearance related to their purpose in your life. Guides who are protective may look like a Roman soldier or an ancient Arabian bodyguard. I've seen guides who appeared as a cartoon character, reminding someone to have fun. Some have a spiritual purpose and may look like a shaman, nun, or wise man. Many guides have had a past life with the person they're watching over and may look like they did in that life.

The spirit guide I communicate with most and call "Chief" appears as an Oglala Sioux Indian, even though we've also had lives together as ancient sailors, homesteaders, and Buddhist monks. His Sioux appearance conveys spiritual wisdom, bravery, and an appreciation for nature, all characteristics that I value greatly. He was my older brother, in our life as Sioux Indians, serving a role similar to his current one as my spirit guide.

Totem Animals

For many Native Americans, meeting their totem animal was an important rite of passage, brought about by a vision quest. Approaching puberty, a brave would venture into the wilderness for days, until he had the anticipated vision. What he learned would be important in determining his direction in life. One of the last chapters in this book describes vision quests in more detail.

In performing clairvoyant readings, my experience has been that most people do have at least one totem animal. We are sometimes subconsciously aware of them, collecting artwork or clothing depicting our totem animal. That was the case for my daughter (dolphin), my sister (bear) and me (wolf). I've also found that although they look like animals, they can communicate in one's native language, give good advice, and serve purposes similar to other spirit guides. Talking to a bear may seem strange, but they do understand. Totem animals are actually advanced spirits who take on the appearance of a particular animal because of the message it conveys. My wolf

displays strength, pride, and a sense of pack, holding family values as very important. He's also an excellent protector.

A friend of mine learned of her horse totem shortly after learning that she had cancer. Seeking spiritual support at a frightening point in her life, she had drummed for a vision, with a small handmade drum, as Native Americans would sometimes do. The horse appeared with rippled muscles and wings, symbolizing tremendous strength. Its message seemed to say, "I will be with you; you can ride on me through this new territory."

During her first visit to the hospital, and with no prompting reason, the nurse asked her if she liked horses. Suddenly, she felt confident that she had found the right place. Over the coming months, as she dealt with treatments, surgery, and doctors' visits, the horse made its presence known again and again, showing up in paintings, a statue, a jacket from Nepal, and embroidered on the pocket of a radiation technician. Each time my friend encountered another symbol of the horse, it reminded her she had love and support from the heavenly realm. She was not alone.

Purposes of Spirit Guides

As mentioned earlier, teaching, protection, and spiritual guidance can be a guide's purpose. Guides may also come into your life to help you learn a musical instrument or sport, remind you to have fun, or help you with healing or with a specific project or problem in your life. Some guides are with you all your life, but special purpose guides may come and go as needed. They may even help you find your glasses or get a good parking space. You just need to ask, and when they help, be sure to thank them.

Before writing this, I asked Chief what else I should include here. He emphasized that in times of trouble or sadness, your guides are always there, listening and ready to help. No matter what, your spirit guides are loving and are very kind in passing any judgment. They understand that you are here on earth learning difficult lessons. When you're happy, laughing, and having fun, your guides are there too, sometimes displaying their own sense of humor. They would, of course, prefer that you are happy, laughing, and having fun.

If you're anxious to contact your angels or guides, go ahead and say something or send a telepathic message. Chapter 8 has an exercise for two-way communication with them.

Final Thoughts

Do you think of yourself as a body that will cease to exist when you die? As a person with a soul? Or as an eternal spiritual being with a temporary body? How does your viewpoint affect your decisions in life? Would thinking differently change your priorities? Would death be less scary?

This is the real world.
~**Chief, spirit guide.**

CHAPTER 4
WE'RE CONNECTED TO ONE
ANOTHER TOO

We are here on earth to learn, to love, and to help one another. Relationships are key. Meditation can improve your relationships as you let go of anger, resentment, judgment, and expectations that get in the way. An additional benefit of meditation is that it's almost impossible to be angry when you're relaxed.

In heaven, spirits remember that they're connected and work eagerly together, helping one another. On earth, we may forget this connection and feel isolated, judgmental, or even hostile toward one another, at least at times. Feeling separate, we make judgments of others or misinterpret their behavior, both of which can lead to anger.

Most of us don't feel separate or judgmental about everyone. We may feel close to our family, friends, or our club, but separate or judgmental towards "them"— whoever "them" is. Maybe it's lazy people, snobbish people, dumb people, fat people, or skinny people. It might be blacks, whites, foreigners, Republicans, or Democrats. What we forget is all those other people are really in our same family or club, the club of spirits with bodies who are on earth learning lessons.

You may find yourself thinking, *how can they be like me? They do such stupid things. Look at how that person drives. It's too fast. It's too slow. It's not like how I drive. How about their hair and their clothes? I'd never dress like that. How can I possibly like salespeople? Rude people? Old people? Young people?*

Complaining about "crappy" drivers and all those other people seems to make some of us feel better, but why? Judging people seems to have its rewards. It's a quick way to sort out and categorize our environment. We might be overwhelmed if we had to deeply analyze everyone we encounter. Judging others often comes from our own insecurity or fear. Our payoff is to feel superior to those whom we judge. The anger that goes with judgment may also give us a false sense of power. This is not where real self-esteem or power comes from, yet most of us have judged others at one time or another. We've also done things that others might judge, possibly even things that seem pretty foolish in hindsight. In fact with all the foolish things I've done, it sometimes amazes me that I lived through my teens.

Okay, we've all done things that others might judge, and almost everyone has negative thoughts about others at times. Why should we change?

One outstanding reason is that you'll feel better. It may seem that when you complain about others, you're "getting it off your chest," and aren't you supposed to unload those negative feelings? This thinking ignores that your negative feelings come from your negative thoughts, which you do have control over. If you control your thoughts in a positive fashion, they will influence your feelings positively. You, and the people around you, will be happier if you work on having positive thoughts.

Another great reason for being positive is that you'll attract more positive things into your life. Energy, matter, and people respond to thought. By being negative, we attract negative people and negative events into our life. Who wants more of that? Positive comments and praise for those around us encourage them to do *more* positive things

If you change the way you look at things, the things you look at change.
~**Wayne Dyer, author,** *The Power of Intention.*

Judging Others

Judging others harshly has been an issue for me. In reviewing my own past lives, I found many spent as a warrior, fighting Indians in one life and as an Indian in the next, and fighting for a variety of armies going back at least a few thousand years. Quick judgments may have served a purpose in survival situations, when a fast decision could mean the difference between life and death. During battle, anger provides the reward of extra strength from adrenaline. But in modern society and on the spiritual plane, these characteristics can get in the way of spiritual growth and relationships. Due to my slow spiritual learning, it's taking me many lifetimes to complete my spiritual lessons.

Along with having a warrior nature to start with, I grew up under circumstances that added to my judgmental and sometimes angry nature. I had high expectations of myself and of life. My father was intelligent, creative, and well educated, almost completing his PhD at a prominent East Coast university. He was also reasonably wealthy, at least when he was young, but he was emotionally unbalanced, lacked confidence in himself, and abused alcohol. After losing two teaching jobs, he spent a number of years drinking and unemployed. My mother finished college, divorced my dad, and raised my sisters and me on a tight budget.

I resented my dad's wasted intelligence and education, concluding that he was just plain lazy. He should have finished his PhD and kept his jobs. Not only did it affect him, but also it deprived me of the more privileged childhood I felt I should have had. Yes, it was self-centered of me to have had such expectations. Along with judging him, I concluded that most people who aren't successful are lazy. As a result, I worked very hard on our appraisal business, and most other things in my life. I sure didn't want to be one of the "lazy" people. Working seventy or more hours a week, I resented so-called lazy people who I felt should get to work and be a success in life. If I worked so hard, why couldn't they?

By angrily resenting "lazy" people, I prevented myself from understanding the bigger picture and caused myself to harbor a great deal of hostility, which didn't feel good. And, of all the times that I became irritated with "lazy" people, I never really changed any of them.

It barely occurred to me that more factors than laziness might be at play. I now realize that many people don't try because they don't believe they can be successful. This may even have been the case with my father. Many don't have the education, the wherewithal, or the ambition. Some people may even have priorities that are vastly different from mine, not caring much about financial success. Was I better off having money but little free time than someone with free time but little money? All that work wasn't much fun. Now, I do feel that working hard isn't necessarily bad. Not working hard isn't necessarily bad either. Finding the proper balance is good, and that balance may not be the same for everyone. Who was I to judge?

On the subject of working hard to obtain wealth, studies have been done on the relation between wealth and happiness. They indicate that people in the middle class tend to be much happier than people who are truly poor. It's hard to be happy when you are barely able to meet your basic needs. However, the same studies indicate that wealthy people are not much happier than those in the middle class. Check any tabloids and you'll see many wealthy people who seem to be downright unhappy. Rather than working constantly toward becoming rich, they might have spent some of their time developing meaningful relationships and enjoying life now. If you work all the time because you love your work, or as part of a bigger plan, then great—go for it. If you subscribe to the theory that "he who dies with the most toys wins," you should probably rethink that one. Once you're dead, nobody will care how many toys you had.

Maybe you don't have an issue with "lazy" people. Do you have a similar attitude about another group? What do you think about Republicans? Democrats? Teenagers? Old people? Salespeople? Crappy drivers? If you're holding onto prejudices against certain groups of people, please consider finding ways to let them go.

Positive Changes

So how do we manage to go around being positive and liking everyone? The truth is that we are *human* and may not be capable of liking everyone we encounter while we're here on earth. Okay, so how do we go about liking and being kind to as many people as possible?

We can try to remember that we're all souls who came from a loving place and are here to learn together. Although we are learning together, we aren't learning the same lesson at the same time. That other person may be working on something that you learned lifetimes ago, or their lesson may be one that you just can't understand from your perspective. They got to where they are very differently, so they may not understand you either. That doesn't make you bad, does it?

There are people in this world who do horrible things, and we may not be enlightened enough yet to forgive everyone, but I do try to remember that it's not my job to judge. That is what laws and the courts are for. There are rules and policing of behavior in the spirit world too.

People take different roads seeking fulfillment and happiness. Just because they're not on your road doesn't mean they've gotten lost.
~Dalai Lama, coauthor, *Art of Happiness.*

Gratitude

Being grateful for what we have goes a long ways toward being positive. It's hard to be negative while you're thankful. All of us have things or people in our life who are a blessing. If you can't think of any, look harder. Just being here and being alive is a blessing.

It's easy to get caught up in dwelling on what we don't have, what we're lacking. We think we'll be happy at some point in the future, once we get whatever it is we want. Once we get it, we may have already thought of something new that is going to make us even happier, further into the future. "My high-tech gizmo is good, but they're already coming out with a new one that's faster, smaller, and cooler. I sure wish I had that one." If *instead*, we are thankful for what we already have, we could be happy now.

To put this into practice when you do find a negative thought pops into your mind, quickly replace it with a pleasant, optimistic thought. If you continue to do this, you'll condition yourself to be pleasant and optimistic, at least most of the time. Once it becomes your predominant way of thinking, staying positive will become easier and your life will be much happier. We all have bad days, or suffer traumatic events, and it's only human to be angry or sad sometimes. The challenge is to not remain in that state, but to let it go and move on. Affirmations can be a powerful tool for accomplishing this. By repeating a positive affirmation, you help your subconscious to learn to be positive. Try phrases like, "I am happy and at peace," "I am well liked," "I am successful at this," or "All is well in my life."

Hard Lessons

If you're resisting much of this because you feel like you've been the victim of horrible circumstances, it can help to be aware that much of what happens to us is a choice that our "higher self" made, in order for us to learn important lessons. Our worst hardships are often our most important sources of growth. We might also have smaller mishaps to remind us to get back on track.

In performing clairvoyant readings, I've seen many instances of someone manifesting an injury or illness due to a lesson they have to learn. Many of these lessons are related to the way this person treats others in their life; for instance, they may develop a life-threatening illness in order to learn compassion for others in a similar circumstance.

A number of years ago, I had two accidents involving torn ligaments within a month. If I'd caught on to the message—that I should slow down and tune into my spirituality more—I might have avoided the second accident.

Connected to Others Meditation

To reinforce your awareness of connectedness, try this visualization meditation. With a stronger awareness of this connection, you'll be naturally inclined to act and feel positively towards your fellow human beings.

Once you're situated in a comfortable, quiet place, take a few deep breaths and relax. Imagine a small alpine lake with boulders along its shore and a glass-smooth surface that reflects the surrounding mountains. You're sitting on a warm, flat boulder, in the middle of the lake. Reaching down, you dip your hand into the cool water of the lake, becoming aware that the water represents the world and its people. Your touching the water signifies your energy and its effect on others. Ripples flow out from your hand, like your actions and deeds flow out into the world. As they reach the boulder-lined shore, some of the ripples gently bounce back, the way your treatment of others comes back to you. Feel this and know that it's the good things you'd like to have returning to you.

Having felt your impact on others, let go of the alpine lake image and become aware of where you are right now. Who is physically closest to you? Is there more than one person? Become aware of and feel the energy field connecting you, like imaginary water in the Quantum Ocean or the alpine lake. Imagine currents and ripples in the energy field flowing out from you to those that are closest, then to neighbors and continuing on out through your city and beyond. Some of those bounce off certain people and come back to you.

This exercise may help to remind you that the good deeds that you do, or the warmth that you show to another, may inspire them to want to do the same for someone else. The effect of each act has the potential to grow and to make the world a more positive and joyous place.

Example

In the office where Jan works, she greets her colleagues with a smile and takes a real interest in how each of their lives is going. After chatting with her, they feel more cheerful and more inclined to treat

one another the same way, making the office a happier place. When her colleagues go home, they greet their families warmly, making their home environment more pleasant. Some of these family members may even take that cheerfulness with them the next day when they go off to work or school, and Jan finds that her coworkers seem happy to see her when they return to work.

Improving Our Closest Relationships

The people who we're closest to and who are the most important to us, such as spouses, mates, families, and close friends, can also be the ones we treat the worst. We may take them for granted or assume that they will always be there, no matter how we treat them.

> *There's one sad truth in life I've found*
> *While journeying east and west.*
> *The only folks we really wound*
> *Are those we love the best.*
> *We flatter those we scarcely know,*
> *We please the fleeting guest,*
> *And deal full many a thoughtless blow*
> *To those who love us best.*
> ~Ella Wheeler Wilcox (1850-1919), author and poet.

When you're around someone a lot, it's easy to notice their faults. Since you're more comfortable around them, you're inclined to point out their faults and get into an argument.

You may think, *how else am I going to get them to change? Besides, when they're being so irritating, they deserve to hear about it, right? It's certainly not my fault that they're so sensitive. If they'd just listen, we wouldn't have to have this big fight.*

Warrior in Action

Maybe that doesn't sound like you, but it unfortunately sounds like me during much of my life, and I could still stand to work on it. I usually am warm, positive, and easy to get along with. In the past, however, my warmth ended when someone did something I deemed rude or unfair—then look out! I sure wasn't going to put up with that. Once irritated or mad, my warrior mode would kick into action. Arguing was like a contest I had to win.

My wife is a bit of a warrior too, so we've had some big arguments over stupid little things, which were often just misunderstandings. Before long, I wouldn't even remember what had started the argument. Sometimes, I'd even goad her into reminding me, so I could properly continue the fight. It didn't really matter what it was about anyway, as long as she apologized and I could declare myself the winner. Another of my favorite techniques was to be sure to stay mad longer than the other person. Surely, that helped prove I was right.

I foolishly applied these same techniques to my teenaged daughters. They can yell pretty loudly, and they're often reluctant to apologize or see what they did wrong. Even worse, they had learned to use some of my techniques on me, and it's no fun being on the receiving end. All that yelling back and forth doesn't help adolescent self-esteem much either.

All those times I thought I was winning, my opponents and I really were both losing. At the end of the argument, we both felt worse than before it started. We rarely accomplished anything, and I certainly didn't gain any friends that way. Luckily, my family usually managed to remember that I'm kind and loving, most of the time.

Arguments and Anger

In an argument, the combatants may feel that they have good reason for their contribution to the fight: *It's important to get my feelings out. If I don't set them straight, they're never going to change. I sure can't let them walk all over me. Besides, I'm so damn mad that I can't help myself. The way they treated me is just not fair. I'm not going to take their crap.*

Personally, I've had all of these thoughts. They can seem like great excuses for having harmful interactions, and to make matters worse, getting angry

can actually feel good. It rewards you with a stimulating shot of adrenaline, along with a false sense of power. Many people even view anger as an admirable, tough, macho thing.

However, like indulging in an addictive drug, it's not worth it. That anger and adrenaline is a leading cause of heart disease. It can also destroy relationships and lead to loneliness. Not only that, but it can lead to violence and bad karma, seriously hampering your spiritual advancement.

If, like me, some part of you has thought that getting mad makes you tough and macho, please rethink that. In a threatening or frustrating situation, it takes more bravery to stand firmly without lashing out in anger. Like cornered animals, people often lash out because they're afraid. Instead, follow the footsteps of Kwai Chang Kaine from the TV show Kung Fu. He never got mad and only fought when he needed to defend himself, or to protect someone in need of help. (I will admit that seemed to happen a lot. It was a television show, after all.)

Holding your hostile thoughts inside is not the answer. It is important to get your feelings out, but fighting or screaming at another person is not the way to do it. You may have noticed that the other person isn't that receptive to hostility anyway.

If you have felt that you need to set someone straight, so they will change, there are better ways to accomplish that. In fact, maybe you've heard the saying, "that which we resist persists." I've found that there are people in our lives that want any kind of attention they can get. If you yell and scream, arguing with them not to do something, they seem awfully inclined to keep doing whatever it is that irritates you so much. If instead, you focus on the positive things that they do, they seem to want to do more positive things. Who would've guessed?

You might also consider that everyone has a right to be their own person. Should you be trying to change them in the first place? If someone's behavior pushed your buttons and got you irritated or infuriated, the following exercise will help in releasing some anger.

Cooling-Down Visualization Meditation

Meditating before you continue an argument is a wise idea. It gives you a chance to cool down and see things from a more logical and healthy perspective, rather than letting anger cloud your judgment. Any meditations in this book can help you learn to stay calm and relaxed, but this exercise is especially helpful for times when you're already angry.

Do you remember the Nature Photo Visualization Meditation, where you placed yourself in a scene of your choice? This exercise has a specific scene for you, although you may certainly modify it to your liking.

Once you're comfortably seated with your eyes closed, visualize yourself walking downhill on a trail through an alpine meadow. It's a warm summer day, and you can feel the sun's heat adding to the heat of your anger. You come to a creek scattered with boulders in and alongside it. Just upstream, a shallow pool opens out at the base of a cliff, with a small waterfall cascading into it. Stand on the creek's bank and feel how hot the sun and your temper are making you. Your skin feels as if it may be turning red with the heat. Go ahead and let this heat build for a short while.

When you're ready to cool down, see yourself stepping into the creek's pool. You can almost feel your skin sizzle as you enter the water. Sit down into the pool with the waterfall showering down on you. The cool water is refreshing, as it carries away the heat and your anger. Sense it all washing downstream, while you relax in the rejuvenating water. Imagine the sound from the falls and the running creek. The air is incredibly fresh and damp with spray. Sit for a few moments and take some deep, clearing breaths.

When you're ready, step out of the creek's pool. You can rest on a boulder, or walk back up the trail and end your visualization.

Example

Margaret's teenaged daughter Susie stayed out all night and never called home. When Margaret confronted her, demanding to know where she had been, Susie responded, "It's no big deal. I'm sixteen years old and can take care of myself. Why don't you mind your own business?"

At that point, Margaret felt her face getting warm. She was ready to lay into Susie but good. She then remembered many similar screaming matches, which never seemed to accomplish anything. Susie almost seemed to enjoy them, but Margaret certainly didn't. This time, instead of blowing up, she walked to the den to try the cool-down visualization. After meditating, she would work on enforcing some logical consequences to Susie's behavior and perhaps even try to have a civilized conversation about why it was not okay to stay out all night. Margaret might point out the fear that it caused her, worrying over Susie's safety.

Assertive versus Aggressive

You should not allow anyone to "walk all over you," but there is a difference between being assertive and being aggressive. It is possible to state your point while still respecting the other person's opinions and their right to have them. The middle of an argument is a good time to step back and look at what you're trying to accomplish and if it's worth what you're going through. You may conclude that harmony with the person you're yelling at is more important than the point you're trying to make. Often, your anger may not even have anything to do with the argument. It may be that you're stressed out about, angry over, or afraid of something else that's going on in your life. That person in front of you just happened to be a handy place to dump your negative emotions. "I'm so mad that I can't help myself" may seem true at the time. The fact is that if you really wanted to, you could help yourself.

This is where meditation can be of great benefit, especially once it becomes a regular habit. The more you meditate, the more you'll find that you can achieve a calm focus that will carry over into all aspects of your life, such as when you're arguing. At the onset of a potential argument, you may even want to take a break and meditate for fifteen minutes. By the time you return, the pointlessness of the whole thing may become apparent. If the other person still wants to fight, suggest that they go meditate for fifteen minutes too. They'll love that one.

If you can't get away for the fifteen minutes, at least stop and take a few deep breaths. Relax and examine what you're doing as objectively as possible. Don't let your emotions take over. Looking deeper, you may realize that although you're arguing with your husband, it's your boss who is causing the frustration in your life. Your husband just seemed safer and more convenient to vent on.

Perfect Pictures

In psychic work, there is a term called *perfect pictures*. That sounds like something really good, like the kind of photography I'd like to take. Actually perfect pictures can cause a lot of trouble and can often set us up for disappointments. A perfect picture is an idealized view of how you'd like something or someone to be. For example, you might expect yourself to always speak perfectly in front of an audience.

Having perfect pictures for ourselves can be a strong motivator, but it can also be a source of poor self-esteem. Many people can't live up to their perfect pictures, such as women who look at models in magazines and have a (perfect) mental image of how they themselves should look. But who can compete with air-brushed models?

If a husband has the same sort of expectation for his wife, that too could cause problems. Our perfect pictures for others can lead to many arguments. Even perfect pictures about what dinner should be like can be enough to start a fight. It is common to have preconceived expectations of how someone should be. These preconceived ideas may not be who they really are, only the person who you expect them to be. Maybe your son doesn't want to be a nuclear physicist or a surgeon. Maybe your daughter truly loves the aspiring rock star and doesn't want to marry the nice lawyer down the street. Maybe your wife's not interested in being the perfect homemaker. If they don't want to listen to you, you probably can't make them.

Please consider letting go of some of those perfect pictures. You'll have more satisfaction and find it easier to get along with others.

Releasing Perfect Pictures

If perfect pictures are causing trouble in your life, this exercise will help you release some of their energy. Start with a relaxation exercise or warm-up meditation. When you're ready, visualize the sort of scene or image that is causing you trouble. See it as if it were a photo, a two-dimensional image.

At this point, you have two options. You can visualize this photo exploding, releasing the energy with a pop. If that sounds too dramatic, use your imagination to create a grounding cord which extends from the corner of the picture down to the center of the earth. Visualize the energy from the picture running down this cord, until the picture shrivels and fades away. The next chapter will provide more information on grounding. Either technique will release and neutralize the energy from these "perfect pictures."

Example

Roger eats a balanced diet and exercises three times a week. He's in good health, but his midsection stays soft and larger than he'd like it to be. When his wife assures him that he looks great for his age, the remark just irritates him. *Do I need to be reminded how old I am?*

While meditating, he examined the situation and realized the problem. He continued to compare himself to the Roger from years ago who ran on the college track team. Roger put that old image into a picture and blew it up. He might still like to lose some weight, but it would be wise to quit expecting to look the same as he'd looked twenty years earlier.

Another Example

As a newlywed, Tonya felt a real issue building in her new marriage. Larry, her husband, spent a couple of hours out in the garage, at least three nights a week, tinkering with his old motorcycle. These were not the candlelit dinners and romantic evenings she had expected. To make matters worse, the more she yelled at Larry, the more he retreated to the garage.

While meditating, Tonya saw that her perfect pictures were at least part of the problem. While she didn't feel right about exploding an image of a romantic candlelit dinner, she was okay with draining the energy from it. Intuition told her that the best solution was a compromise. She'd let go of expecting romance every night, and she'd talk to Larry nicely about reducing his time in the garage.

Improving Relationships

Here are some additional steps we can take to improve our relationships. If we do, we'll be happier, the people around us will be happier, and it will be easier to meditate.

- Learn to love and accept yourself. Once you do, it will be much easier to love and accept other people. Let go of perfect pictures.
- Listen to the other person, asking questions about their life.
- Try to understand their point of view. It may be different from yours, but that doesn't necessarily make it wrong. It might be that if

you actually understood their point of view, you wouldn't be angry in the first place. Many fights start with a misunderstanding. Chapter 8 will help with this.

- Be honest with the other person, and with yourself. It's hard to have a great relationship without trust.
- Learn to compromise.
- Forgive. Holding onto anger and resentment makes you miserable and doesn't prove anything. It can also lead to illness.
- Share the work and the fun. The other person undoubtedly wants to have fun too, rather than be saddled with all the work. Fun activities can help keep the spark alive in a relationship.
- Don't sweat the small stuff. Once you realize this is just one of many lives, it almost all becomes small stuff.
- *Meditate!* I know I've already mentioned this one, but stress is a big block to good relationships. It makes it harder to think, feel, and communicate. If you can accurately read (understand) other people, you're much less inclined to get mad. Many fights start over a silly miscommunication.
- Encourage others to meditate. If they're full of stress, it naturally leads to all the issues noted above.

Meditating and connecting with your spiritual side makes it easier to do all of these things. You'll find that by using these techniques regularly, your relationships will get better and better. The following exercise can speed up the process.

Improving Relationships Meditation

This meditation will increase your positive feelings towards those around you. Once you've reached your quiet and comfortable place, take a few deep breaths and relax. With your thoughts quieted, visualize a very important person in your life. This could be a spouse, child, parent, or close friend. Holding their image, contemplate one or two traits that are unique and positive about them. Maybe they're very generous, creative, funny, or loving. If positive characteristics are not coming up, remember that person is only human and move through their traits until you find a positive one. Everyone has some. As you're contemplating that trait, feel your fondness for that person. The feeling is probably coming from the area of your heart or fourth chakra.[9] After feeling the warmth for that person, find someone else important in your life and do the same thing.

As you move from person to person, sense a growing golden glow radiating from your heart, like sunshine. Let the rays of this warmth shine for as long as you like, touching the important people in your life. If you want, you can then expand it farther so it reaches others—those in your neighborhood and town, or even the world. If everyone did this, we could make the world a brighter, more loving place. When you're done, take a few more deep breaths and realize that you can continue to radiate that caring light as you go on about your day.

---

9   Chakras, or the seven energy centers in our bodies, will be described in more detail in chapter 5 – Grounding and Neutrality.

Final Thoughts

We are here on earth learning lessons together. If all of us were the same, how much would we learn?

It is the things in common that make relationships enjoyable, but it is the little differences that make them interesting.
~ Todd Ruthman, author.

CHAPTER 5
GROUNDING AND NEUTRALITY

You can create your own personal grounding cord from quantum energy. Grounding allows you to release anxiety, stress, pain, anger, fear, and other negative energy that may be blocking your optimal health and happiness. Your personal grounding also gives you a strong connection to the earth and helps your body feel secure, as you bring more energy in and run it through your own energy system.

If you're well grounded, you'll be less likely to be troubled by life's bumps in the road, and less susceptible to other people's grouchiness, clumsiness, or anger. We've all met very ungrounded people who are stressed, angry, or absent-minded. In fact, I came across an example in the fast-food line recently at Wendy's. While reaching for his large soda, a customer in front of me managed to flip his pop over onto the counter. The plastic lid held, so only a little pop spilled onto the counter. After the manager got that wiped up, the customer over-eagerly lifted his tray and tipped the pop onto the floor, where it broke apart and made a big, sticky mess. At that point, his faced turned red and his gestures became more animated, like the scarecrow in *The Wizard of Oz*. I stepped back and grounded myself, wanting to stay out of the growing disaster in front of me.

The grounding exercise that we'll cover in this chapter, will help you avoid becoming a part of such mishaps. It's also an effective first step to any meditation. You can even reinforce your grounding throughout the day without meditating. It only takes a second to make a quick check that your grounding is intact and solid by visualizing your connection. This is especially important at times when you're feeling anxious, stressed, or downright angry.

Chakras and the Aura

A basic understanding and awareness of the chakras and aura can be helpful for grounding and for some other meditations. With this knowledge, you can increase the energy flow through them and gain insight into what you're using that energy for.

You may already be familiar with an aura. It is a field of energy that surrounds the human body. Actually, animals, plants, rocks, and most other things have some sort of aura. Most Native Americans believed that the earth and all things on it have a spirit, which in a sense they do. Like everything else, auras are part of that larger energy field, the Quantum Ocean. Most people's auras extend out about one or two feet from their bodies; however, this can vary considerably. Jesus, Mohammed, Buddha, and other spiritual leaders were said to have vast auras, while other people may unconsciously keep their auras very close to their bodies.

The chakras are energy centers within your aura. There are many chakras, but the seven main chakras that line up with the spinal column are the ones people usually refer to. Each of these corresponds to a layer of your aura and an aspect of your life. Chakras contain a great deal of information, and like the aura, can be a valuable source of information in psychic readings. The images and symbols that a clairvoyant sees in your aura usually pertain to what is currently going on in your life, while the chakras contain information that is an integral part of you, like your past-life memories. A strong connection exists between the condition of your chakras and your emotional, physical, and spiritual well-being. Emotional issues like trauma or anger can lead to a block in your chakras, and a block in your chakras can lead to health issues and other troubles.

Chakras are somewhat cone shaped, with the wider part toward the front of your body. Energy typically flows in the front and out the back. They vary in degrees of how open or closed they are, and this can change over the course of a day. You can even learn to open or close them through intention. Visualize a gauge in front of the chakra that you're adjusting, so you can check the percentage of openness. Then just visualize the chakra opening or closing, while the gauge moves to the level you desire. If you're having a hard time visualizing this, just know that your thoughts can create your reality. If you simply intend for it to happen, it will be so.

Here is a brief description of each of the seven main chakras.

The first chakra is located near the base of your spine. It has been called the "survival chakra" and has information related to things like money, work, security, and home. When someone is panicked or in fear, this chakra may be wide open. Closing this chakra down to 30 percent or less can help calm those feelings, while still allowing an adequate energy flow. Someone who is constantly fearful may have an energy block in this chakra, that disrupts that energy flow. While you're meditating, you can close the first and second chakras down to approximately 10 percent. This helps you reach a calm, meditative state. When you're done meditating, consider readjusting these first two chakras to the 30 percent range.

The second chakra is located slightly below your navel. It contains energy and information related to emotions and sexuality. Old emotional issues can cause blocks in this chakra, which could lead to an explosive temper, manipulative behavior, sexual addiction, or other emotionally related problems.

The third chakra is located in the solar plexus, just below the ribs. It is related to personal power, self-esteem, and your ability to obtain goals. This is an important chakra to have open (approximately 80%) and flowing. Blockages can lead to low energy and being unable to achieve what one wants to in life.

The fourth chakra is your heart chakra, located in the center of your chest. It is related to your affinity with yourself and others. Love and caring come from this one. Damage to this chakra leads to fear of getting hurt or feeling unworthy of love. Leave the fourth and fifth chakras 50 to 60 percent open most of the time.

The fifth is your communication chakra, which also relates to creativity. It is located at the base of your throat. As you may have guessed, blockages can lead to difficulty in creating and communicating what you intend.

The sixth chakra, or "third eye," is located just above the bridge of your nose, the place you've seen some people wear a red dot. This chakra is related to clairvoyance or, translated from French, "clear seeing." Blockages make it difficult to see what is going on with others or to tell a truth from a lie.

Clairvoyants use this chakra for seeing images during a psychic reading. If you're meditating and accessing psychic information, you might want this chakra 80 percent open. Sixty percent open is reasonable for daily life.

The seventh, or "crown chakra," is located at the top of your head. It is related to intuition (psychic knowing) and provides a connection to information from your higher self and to the universe. Blockages in this chakra make it difficult to access your intuition and spiritual information. As a form of protection, when doing psychic readings, it is wise to keep your seventh chakra closed down to the 15 percent range. This still allows an adequate flow of energy and doesn't impede receiving psychic information. Around thirty percent open is fine most of the time.

Releasing Energy

Now that you have some background on the aura and chakras, you can apply this information to grounding. Energy responds to thought, and energy in a non-solid form responds immediately to thought. So when you imagine a grounding cord, you are actually creating one. Your grounding cord could take any of many shapes, like a rope, tree root, chain, column of light, or perhaps a fiber-optic cable. The cord should extend from your first chakra, at the base of your spine, all the way down to the center of the earth. Your grounding cord will pass through any substance, manmade or natural—buildings, air, water, rock—so you can use it anywhere.

Grounding Meditation

You can use this simple exercise to put grounding into practice, and it is a form of meditation. Initially, it's easiest on a chair, in a quiet room, where you won't be disturbed. Close your eyes and relax. Take a few deep breaths, exhaling slowly. Now imagine the grounding cord of your choice, such as a thick fiber-optic cable, extending from the base of your spine straight down to the center of the planet. Imagine what the cable looks like and what the connection feels like. Gravity is drawing any negative energy out of you, clearing your aura, and releasing it down your cord. Decide what you want to release, and encourage it to go.

If annoying thoughts are popping into your head, they may be part of the energy you're releasing. You can sometimes see the darker energy on its way out; otherwise, just try to sense the energy as it makes its way down. Maybe that dark energy around your third chakra is from arguments with your boss, or maybe it's old energy from your parent's disappointment with you, due to their perfect pictures. Let go of it, and watch it drain out. If it seems difficult because you're trying too hard, let your effort go down the cord too.

The molten heat at the center of the earth will change any negative energy back to pure energy, and then it can return to its source. So if you're releasing negative energy from a fight with a friend, don't feel guilty. The energy will return to them in a neutral form and will not hurt the planet.

As an experiment, you can disconnect your grounding cord and see if you notice a difference. Once you notice the difference, reconnect your grounding cord or establish a new one.

Grounding is something you can use all the time, so go ahead and leave it connected. Once you're comfortable with this technique, you can check it anywhere to make sure you're still grounded—at work, while walking, at the computer, or even while driving. If grounding causes a lot of emotional release for you or induces a meditative trance, of course don't check it while driving. It works fine for me, but we're not all alike.

Grounding Your Environment

When you're inside, grounding your environment releases any negative energy from your room or house. To ground your room, imagine a grounding cord extending from the floor to the center of the earth. Next, imagine a ball of golden energy in the center of the room. Allow it to expand and grow until it fills the entire room, house, or property. The golden energy is of a higher vibration and will help move out anything negative, including energy or even low-level spirits.

Example

At one point, there was an entity hanging around an unused bedroom in our basement. My youngest daughter and I would occasionally notice it as a visible movement of energy or as a wisp of smoke. It wasn't causing trouble, much like when you have a mouse living in your walls. I left it alone for a while, but when we decided to make use of that room, I decided to clear it out with a ball of golden energy.

We haven't seen it since, and my youngest daughter is now living in that room. The spirit had no doubt found some new, quieter place to hang out.

Not only does this technique move out negative energy and some spirits, but bringing up the vibration in the house can have a positive effect on everyone in the house. I use these techniques every day and find them to be very beneficial.

Staying Neutral

Grounding, and releasing any negative energy, will certainly help you stay more neutral. It's hard to reach a calm, meditative state if distracting emotions and thoughts are coming up, such as "Why are my kids always getting into trouble?" By staying grounded and neutral, you can look at the possibility that they aren't always getting into trouble.

So what else can we do to help us stay neutral? We can actually control where we are coming from. By that, I mean we can control where our spiritual center is or where our consciousness is. If we have an out-of-body experience, our spiritual center is out of our body. If we're watching a tear-jerker movie, it is likely to be in our heart area (fourth chakra). When a guy notices a beautiful woman at the bar, his center might be lower, in his second chakra.

Because meditating requires a calm, focused state, it is best to avoid tear-jerker emotions or the sexual feelings of the guy at the bar. Those emotions are fine—at the appropriate times. In order to remain neutral while meditating, the center of your head (the sixth chakra) is related to "clear seeing" and is the best place to be for seeing things objectively and without judgment.

Note that this location is not the same as your analytical mind. The "center of your head" is between and slightly above your eyes, about two inches behind your forehead.

Staying Neutral Exercise

To experience the center of your head, start with the grounding meditation exercise. Begin to sense your **center** *(where you're coming from). This might already be in the center of your head, or it could be in the fourth or second chakra. If it's not already there, try moving your* **center** *to the center of your head. Shift your focus to the center of your head and imagine coming from there. This may not make sense until you experiment with it, and actually feel it. After experiencing the center of your head, try moving your* **center** *to other areas, such as your heart area. You may have experienced this when your "heart goes out to someone." You might also try your second chakra (your emotion chakra), just below your navel. This is where your* **center** *might be when you're overwhelmed with emotion. Notice how each of these locations feels a little different. Then try moving your* **center** *a few inches above your head. You can move your* **center** *to a corner of the room or into your toe. After experiencing that, I'd suggest you return to the center of your head. Don't worry—I'm sure your* **center** *won't stay in your toe.*

Releasing Old Stuff

In my clairvoyant training, we spent many hours staying grounded and centered while we psychically looked at old pictures from our lives, bringing up stuff that could be causing blocks. As we brought up pictures and issues, we would release any unwanted energy down our grounding cords.

This is a great source of spiritual and emotional growth, much like a form of psychotherapy. Releasing these blocks frees up your energy system, allowing it to reach a higher vibrational state. Feel free to try this at home. After reaching a meditative state and connecting your grounding cord, try visualizing yourself at different ages, seeing and remembering what your life was like then. At two years old, who was important in your life? How did they treat you? How did that affect you? Were there any major events around that time in your life? If so, how did they affect you? If some negative emotions come up, release the energy and let it travel down your grounding cord.

Look at the age of five, ten, fifteen, and so on, repeating the questions and steps for each age. Alternatively, you could simply look for major events in your life, moving through them in chronological order and releasing any negative energy from each event.

Example

John meditated and tuned into the age of two. He saw himself tottering across the living room floor, happy to be walking. Then he watched as his four-year-old brother, Brent, tripped him. Immediately John's mother came running to comfort him. John realized that his mom treated him special, as the baby of the family. Brent was jealous and stayed that way all through their childhood.

At the age of fifteen, John saw himself struggling in baseball. Brent played catch with him and gave him pointers, but he was anxious to pick on any mistakes. Yet John also saw that at times, he and Brent were close and looked out for each other.

John examined his relationship with his mother at fifteen. He saw her trying to hug him in front of a group of his friends. To her, he was still the baby of the family, making it difficult for John to be the macho and mature fifteen-year-old he so wanted to be. John looked at how these relationships had affected his life and worked on releasing any leftover, unwanted energy. As he released this, he felt a slight shift in the way he felt about his mother and brother. They were human with strengths and weaknesses, like everyone else. Releasing old resentments gave John a chance to focus more on their positive traits.

John then continued looking at each five-year period of his life, up to his present age of thirty-six.

Using Grounding Every Day

Although I'm no longer in a clairvoyant training program, I still work on grounding every day. Not only is it the first step when I meditate, I also check my grounding regularly. It takes me roughly three seconds and is well worth the time. When I notice a tailgater on my back bumper, or if someone starts shouting at me, I find it very beneficial to take a few deep breaths and make sure my grounding cord is doing its job. I can then usually manage to go about my day without letting these things bother me, whereas at one time I would have continued to stew.

Staying centered and grounded can be an enormous help in getting through all of life's day-to-day difficulties. They work very well when meditating, but you can use these techniques anytime to help you stay more calm and focused. Grounding can also help to release emotional baggage that people sometimes carry with them for years. Letting go of this stuff allows your energy to move freely and releases blocks to emotional, physical, and spiritual well-being.

When I let go of what I am,
I become what I might be.
~Lao Tzu (600 BC-531 BC), founder of Taoism,
author, *Tao Te Ching*.

CHAPTER 6
RUNNING YOUR ENERGIES

Like grounding, running your energies is a very powerful meditation technique that can release blocks to your spiritual, emotional, and physical health. These two techniques, used together, are the most important and beneficial exercises in this book.

We now know that everything is made of energy. That includes you, your house, the earth, the cosmos, and everything else. For maximum health and well-being, your energy should be flowing and renewing itself, constantly replacing the old with the new. If your energy is slow or stuck, it can lead to feeling sluggish and to having health and emotional problems. Imagine how healthy a clean mountain stream is compared to a stagnant, polluted backwater.

Keeping your energy flowing enhances your

immune system and releases blocks. In chapter 1, I mentioned that this is an important purpose of acupuncture, yoga, reiki, tai chi, and other eastern practices. Releasing these blocks and moving energy is also among the most important steps to raising your vibrational level, becoming more psychic, and more connected to your spiritual or higher self.

Exercise increases your energy flow, and exercising outdoors is better yet. For years, I'd start feeling lethargic if I went too long without getting out to kayak, hike, or ski. Now, I can also run my energies by meditating. I still love to get outdoors, and one of my favorite experiences is hiking up a mountain, finding a scenic spot, and meditating. Outdoor exercise is probably not enough to clear all blocks. When combined with meditation, it can be a big help, with other important health benefits.

Earth and Cosmic Energies

The energy I'm speaking of actually consists of earth energy and cosmic energy. Cosmic energy comes from the air, sun, sky, and heavens, entering your body through the top of your head, or seventh chakra. It works best in your upper chakras. Because there are a variety of sources for cosmic energy, there are many types and vibrations of these energies.

Earth energy comes from the earth, and is the denser form of energy. It comes through chakras in your feet and travels up through your legs. (Remember, you have more than the seven main chakras.) Earth energy works best in your lower chakras—the first, second, and third.

Exercise for Running Your Energies

To put this energy movement into practice, you can use the following exercise. Find a chair in a quiet room. Close your eyes and relax, taking a few deep breaths. Connect your grounding cord to your first chakra, at the base of your spine, and let the energy from any negative thoughts or events run down the cord. Make sure that you're in the center of your head before continuing.

Now let your attention turn toward the chakras in the arches of your feet. Allow them to open up, bringing in clean energy, from deep in the earth. Feel the energy's warmth tingling as it travels up through your ankles, calves, and thighs, cleansing everything in its path. You may pick a color for this energy and watch it as it makes its way up. Green or tan are good colors for earth energy, but use whatever color seems natural for you. A brown, muddy color may be too sluggish. If the flow seems to slow or stop along the way, imagine the energy as warm water, melting a block of sugar. This should help get the energy moving through that trouble spot. Reaching the base of your spine, the energy causes your first chakra to spin and glow. Most of the energy then travels from there down your grounding cord, carrying with it any blocks that were in its path.

Some earth energy continues up through your torso and out the top of your head. From there, it runs down your aura, cleansing along the way. It continues to the bottom of your aura, below your feet, where the energy flows into your grounding cord and is carried downward toward the center of the earth.

Now that you have your earth energy running, the next step is to add lighter cosmic energy. Imagine a ball of cosmic energy over your head, formed by drawing energy down from high in the sky. Blue or gold are strong healing and cleansing choices for this energy. Now let it pour gently into the top of your head through your seventh chakra. From there, feel its warmth as it makes its way down through energy channels in your back, alongside your spine. When it reaches your first chakra, let it mix with your earth energy. A little of the cosmic energy will travel down your grounding cord, along with most of the earth energy. Feel the rest of the cosmic energy, mixed with a little earth energy, traveling up channels in the front of your body.

When this mixture reaches your throat chakra, let some split off and travel down your arms, cleansing them and releasing any blocks. Let the rest of this energy travel up to the top or your head and cascade down through your aura. As this energy runs down and cleans your aura, be sure to fill in any thin areas behind you or to your sides. Relax and let this flow continue for ten or more minutes.

After you've practiced this for a few weeks, you might consider adding another step. As the energy travels up your front channels, visualize some of it running through your second chakra, from front to back, then running down your grounding cord. See your chakra spinning brightly and releasing any negative energy. Visualize this energy from your front channels doing the same for your third chakra, then your fourth, fifth, and sixth chakras, with the remaining energy flowing back out through your seventh and down your aura.

I realize that putting this all together is compli-cated, but the more you practice it, the easier it will become and the stronger your energy flow will be. At first, you may want to start with just your earth en-ergy. You may also find that some variation of these instructions works better for you. Be sure to let energy flow without trying to force it. Relax and take a deep breath once in a while. Let any effort go down your grounding cord. You may not always feel the energy moving, but know that your intention is making it so.

Reading and Releasing Energies

Running your energies is worth doing every day. Once you're used to running energy through your chakras, you can occasionally work on "reading" the issues related to each chakra, as you work your way up. This is another self-healing technique for releasing energy blocks.

As your cosmic energy reaches your first chakra, let it run while you tune into any issues related to that chakra. Remember, the first chakra pertains to home, money, school, or survival issues. What is go-ing on in your life related to these issues? Does some old business or trouble immediately come to mind? How do you feel about what's coming up? How have these emotions affected you? Do you feel someone else's energy interfering? Is there something you'd like to change? As you ask each question, relax and let go of effort. Try to stay out of an analytical mode. Let an answer come to you intuitively. As you gently process any thoughts or feelings, keep running energy through

*your first chakra, releasing unwanted energy down
your grounding cord.*

*When you feel your first chakra issues are complete, move up to the second chakra, which pertains to
emotions. Follow the same steps for the second, then
move on to the third chakra and the fourth, making
your way up to the seventh. You can refer back to the
description of each chakra as a reminder of what
each relates to.*

Example

As Lori ran energy through her first chakra, an image began to take shape. She saw an empty bowl on
a table and knew it represented her current lack of
a job, because it caused her to worry about paying
the bills and putting food on the table. Lori had some
savings and plenty of work experience. She felt reasonably confident she'd land a new job soon, but her
current situation definitely caused some fear. She
released some of that fear by visualizing it as darker
energy running down her grounding cord.

Tuned into her second chakra, which pertains
to emotions, Lori saw an image of her dad yelling at
her about a report card. It brought up old feelings
of inadequacy, which losing her job seemed to have
triggered. She worked on releasing the energy from
these emotions. In her third chakra, she saw the
image of a dried raisin, which seemed to represent
her shriveled self-esteem. Lori ran extra energy, to
flush that image out and to renew the vitality of her
third chakra.

In her fourth or heart chakra, Lori saw an image
of her Shetland sheepdog, with his tongue hanging

out and his tail wagging. It immediately brought a feeling of warmth and love to her. Lori continued up through her fifth, sixth, and seventh chakras, taking in information and releasing whatever she wanted to let go of.

Powerful Spiritual Beings

While we may not always feel this way on earth, we are eternal and powerful spiritual beings. Through life's challenges and difficulties, we experience our greatest growth. In our current life, many of us tend to stay well within our comfort zones, avoiding challenges and new experiences, missing wonderful opportunities. Many of us stay in this comfort zone because we lack the confidence to push our limits or try new things.

This meditation exercise will strengthen your sense of true inner power, providing the confidence to venture out and explore your growth zone. With this confidence, you may try new adventures, like camping, signing up for a class, or joining a new group.

You can also use this exercise during difficult or trying times to become more aware of your inner spiritual strength, which will help carry you through life's challenges.

Powerful Being of Light Visualization

Once you're comfortably seated with your eyes closed and your energy running, visualize yourself as an entity of light. This is your true spiritual state. As more bright light pours in through the top of your head, feel it expand your strength and power. You might visualize yourself becoming bigger or brighter. Know and understand that as spirit, you are eternal and powerful, capable of manifesting great things. Feel this strength continue to grow. When you finish your meditation, carry this strength with you as you venture out and face life's many challenges.

Effects of Energy

By increasing your energy flow, you will be flushing out blocks and releasing them through your grounding cord. For the most part, you'll feel much better, but you may find yourself remembering unpleasant experiences, or you may initially go through days of feeling emotional or out of sorts. You may also have strange, vivid dreams or unusual sleep patterns. These symptoms are due to issues coming to the surface. In clairvoyant training, they refer to this as a *growth period*. Use this time as an opportunity to examine issues and then let them go. It is a normal part of the process and is very healing. Continue to meditate. You'll get through this quicker if you ground and run your energies more to finish releasing whatever is coming up for you.

Whatever you're releasing will pass, and you'll soon find yourself feeling happier, healthier and more at peace. Grounding and running your energies are such powerful and important exercises that I start all my meditation sessions with these steps. As you let go of blocks in your energy system, you'll become more like the loving spirits of heaven. You may also start to notice an increase in psychic experiences, which can be very useful for making decisions and understanding other people. The more often and longer you do these exercises, the greater your benefit will be.

The higher your energy level, the more efficient your body, the more efficient your body, the better you feel and the more you will use your talent to produce outstanding results.
~**Anthony Robbins, author,** *Awaken the Giant Within.*

CHAPTER 7
ENERGY HEALING

In grounding and running your energies, you've learned powerful meditation techniques for healing yourself. Using a similar method, you can help other people to move energy and release blocks, so they too can heal themselves. Along with this easy technique, we'll cover some simple exercises for dealing with specific ailments.

Ways to Heal

Certainly, one option for helping others to heal is to buy or lend them a copy of this book and encourage them to meditate themselves. The person who needs healing most may resist meditation for a number of reasons. Not everyone is ready for the enlightenment that meditation might bring them. Or it may be that you don't know them very well, but you know that they need healing. They may not be in a condition to meditate, or you may find that some people think you're nuts and don't want to discuss any of this with you. I get that regularly. Whatever the reason, sometimes it's just easier to work on healing them yourself. You can use the following technique with the healee sitting in front of you, or you can use it long distance. Use the person's name or image to make a connection. Like a phone conversation, it's possible to work with energy over long distances. I've done many readings and healings for people a thousand or more miles away.

I always first ask for permission from them or telepathically from their spiritual/higher self, which is usually much more enlightened and cooperative than their human persona. It is possible that even on a spiritual level, some people don't want to be healed. They may have a karma issue, or they may have manifested the illness for a lesson they have yet to learn. It may even be that at some level, they see the illness as beneficial, garnering attention or giving them an excuse not to work. It can be difficult to heal someone who doesn't want to be healed, and you shouldn't force healing on anyone.

If you're healing from a distance and don't want to call them for permission, you can communicate telepathically. Meditate first, then visualize the person and their name to make contact. Ask your question silently (think it), calmly listening for an answer. If you get a strong sense of "no," discontinue the process and move on to another exercise. The vast majority of people, at least on a spiritual level, are very appreciative of any help. You're probably not going to hear a loud "yes," but if you get a sense that they'd appreciate it, then go ahead.

Performing the Healing

First, I would recommend grounding and running your own energies, as described in the previous chapters. If the other person isn't sitting in front of you, say hello telepathically. Tell them what you want to do, and ask for their permission. Once you get a go-ahead, picture a simple image of their body. Just as you did for yourself, connect a grounding cord to their first chakra and visualize them releasing any negative energy. From that point, you can follow the same steps for them that you followed to run your own energies, or you can simply picture a big ball of healing energy (blue, gold, or a color of their choice) washing over them. Watch it pour blobs of clean energy all over them, melting away any blocks or sickness, which then flush down their grounding cord and are replaced with fresh, healthy energy. Run this until all of their energy seems clean and renewed.

Once you're finished, you don't have to shut the energy off. I even suggest to the healee's higher self that they continue to keep the energy running as long as they want, and that they do this anytime they'd like. You can then thank them for the opportunity to practice this. Perhaps your healee will thank you at this point, or maybe they'll just look at you strangely and head for the door. Either way, your healing will do them a great deal of good.

I use this technique at least a few times a week, applying it to whomever I feel could use it the most. Recipients have included my children, mother, siblings, and in-laws, along with any friends or acquaintances who are having problems in their lives. After doing a few healings, I have found that their lives seem to improve, or there is a shift and they get past whatever the problem was. Healing doesn't always mean a physical cure. Often, the purpose of a healing is to release emotional blocks or to help prepare someone for a smoother transition to the afterlife.

Performing a healing is also beneficial to the person who gives it—the healer. You meditate longer, and it gets your own energy moving in the process. Not to mention that it's good for your karma, and it may make the other person easier to get along with.

Simplified Healing

Use a special energy of your healee's color choice, and run it much like you run cosmic energy. Imagine it filling the recipient's body and renewing any damaged areas or cells needed for optimal health.

Example

Steve's sister, Liz had just learned that her husband was leaving her for another woman. Liz was in emotional turmoil and emphatically informed Steve that she did not care to talk about it. He didn't bother discussing energy healing because as a very traditional person, Liz thought Steve's spiritual practices were weird.

Steve sat down and reached a meditative state. He contacted Liz's higher self, who he found to be much more open-minded about receiving some energy healing. Steve worked with Liz's higher self, psychically explaining what he was doing as he helped her run her energies and release some of her grief and anger.

During the next week, Steve did this two more times. Although Liz wasn't consciously aware of the healings, the releasing made her feel better and more in control of her life. The following weekend, Liz called to talk to him and share some of her feelings. Although she was still very upset, Steve sensed that Liz had released a great deal of negative energy and was in a much better place than before the healings. Liz even asked Steve how his meditating was going. Eventually, she would move on with her life and heal.

Other Healing Techniques

The technique I described can be enormously helpful, and can support any medical treatment someone is receiving. But, please don't quit going to the doctor. These techniques work well along with the medical treatment that a person may need.

Many other healing techniques help release blocks and increase your energy flow, such as Reiki, acupuncture, healing touch, qigong, and more. Visualization exercises for healing are very powerful because they can do even more than move quantum energy. Using quantum mechanics, visualization can change the structure of cells, which are made of energy, repairing or removing damaged tissue. On earth, energy's response to thought is not as immediate as it is in the spirit world, so be persistent and patient in your visualizations. Visualization also helps trigger the body's natural ability to heal by providing more of what you need such as increasing blood flow or ramping up your immune system. To get this physical response, it's best if the person in need of healing does some of the visualizing. If they don't wish to cooperate with you, try working with their "higher self," speaking to them telepathically while you perform the visualization.

In using visualizations for healing, you can get creative and experiment, finding what works best for you and for the given ailment. Follow your intuition. It can help to read up on the condition, so you can better understand and visualize the necessary repairs or changes the body needs to make. The important points are to let go of any blame, imagine positive results, and believe that the repairs will happen (or better yet have already happened). There are countless cases of people overcoming an illness through energy healing, prayer, willpower, and faith. Below you'll find some examples of visualizations you can start with.

Healing Visualizations

For each of these visualizations, grounding and running your own energies is a wise way to start. If the healing is for someone else, it would be beneficial to make sure the recipient is grounded, and you can work on running their energies too. This will help them release blocks and anything else that is hampering their health.

Cuts or Wounds

For a cut or other skin wound, visualize the white blood cells engulfing and carrying away any bacteria, preventing infection. Then see the cells that make up the skin and muscle multiplying and repairing the wound. Visualize the area changing and growing together until it's free of injury. Imagine and see the healthy new skin as clearly as possible.

Broken Bones

Just as you did for the cut, see your cells multiplying and knitting a broken bone back together. Imagine calcium crystals filling in the damaged areas. Visualize the bone changing until it's straight and strong. For cuts or broken bones, you might also consider using a metaphorical visualization. For example, you could visualize making a repair with superglue, plastering a crack in a wall, sewing skin back together, removing damaged cells with a vacuum cleaner, or using whatever visualization comes to mind.

Hypertension or Arteriosclerosis

For hypertension, any visualization will improve the condition by teaching your body and mind to relax. A visualization to improve your arteries could consist of visualizing them wide-open with blood moving through easily. Visualize cholesterol dissolving away, leaving blood vessels smooth and clean.

In applying the power of thought, here are a few more techniques you can use. Once in a meditative state, visualize any diseased cells as specks or spots in the body. With your focused intention, see them change into healthy cells. See this taking place throughout the body until all the cells are renewed and healthy.

Cancer

Cancer is an uncontrolled growth of abnormal cells in the body. It starts with a single abnormal cell in your body. Normally your immune system's white blood cells will detect such a cell, then engulf and destroy it. If, for some reason, your immune system doesn't manage to do its job, cancer can start to grow. Stress and negative emotions tend to suppress the immune system and make a person more susceptible to cancer. Meditation can help prevent cancer in the first place. For a person who's working to recover from cancer, it can help to stimulate the immune system and tap into the power of quantum physics. For the cancer patient, it's important to reduce stress, so meditation would be especially beneficial.

To activate the immune system, visualize powerful white blood cells eating the weaker cancer cells. You could picture white blood cells as a vast army attacking and destroying the fragile cancer cells, or picture your white blood cells as Pacmen gobbling up the abnormal cells. See whatever remnants the white blood cells leave behind being carried to the kidney or liver and flushed out of body as waste. Only strong healthy cells are left behind. These search-and-destroy exercises could be followed with an exercise to bring in new energy.

Healing in Action

My wife, Mary, specialized in healing work during a number of her past lives, and she does some healing work in her current life. One afternoon, we got a call requesting a long-distance healing. The caller's friend was in a coma and in critical condition, with a severe staph infection and pneumonia. He was on a ventilator and on full-time dialysis. His prospect for survival was poor.

Together, Mary and I performed a reading and healing, working especially hard on the damaged areas of his body. Immediately following the healing session, Mary received a message from the spirit world (a voice in her head) suggesting that she should keep doing healings on this man every day for a week. She performed healings daily, running healing energy throughout his body, especially to his lungs, brain, and other organs. Other techniques also came to her such as energetically pounding on his lungs to break up and loosen the congestion.

Exactly one week later, we got a call saying the man had come out of the coma and his dialysis had been reduced to just three hours a day. His recovery went more quickly than expected, and he was soon released from the hospital. His medical treatment undoubtedly had a lot to do with his recovery, as did the prayers of friends and family, but we're confident that Mary's healings also played a large part in his recovery. Of the four similar cases in Minnesota that year, he was the only one who survived. He reported that his doctors have been amazed to find that he's had no debilitating side effects.

A few months after this man's recovery, I spoke to him and learned that during his coma, he had technically died twice. He had also awoken with the memory of some very moving spiritual experiences. At one point, he was on a plain with a Native American who was trying to give him a message. He also remembered a woman coming into the room whom he seemed to know.

Mary did another reading for him and learned that the Native American was one of his spirit guides, telling him that he was getting a second chance and that he needed to return to his body. The woman was his deceased mother, whom he had been very close to. She was there to provide comfort. At the time, she hadn't made her identity clear because she wanted to make sure he finished his work on earth rather than accompanying her to heaven.

Since that time, this man has experienced many of his own clairvoyant visions, including catching occasional glimpses of spirits around him. One sunny day outdoors with friends, he commented on a circling group of eagles that apparently no one else could see. His spirit guide reported to Mary that both of these events were to remind him of his spiritual nature and to stay on a path that emphasized being good to, and spending time with, the important people in his life.

Emotional Healing

Mary, as a recipient this time, received a healing to move an emotional block. While she was in a class studying energy healing, another student practiced a technique on her. Working on the third chakra, which is related to personal power and self-esteem, the fellow student noticed unusual heat coming from that chakra, indicating a possible block. She worked on moving energy through it until the heat dissipated. At the time, Mary felt some kind of shift. After class, she sat in her car and began feeling emotions rising up for no apparent reason, and she began to cry. Images from a high school relationship with an abusive boyfriend started popping up. She'd identified the source of her third chakra block. After she had released this block, I noticed her to change, becoming more confident and happier. Like me, she works on releasing more old stuff and continues to grow and heal. It is great to see.

Final Thoughts

The techniques in this chapter are a good starting point. There are many forms of energy healing that you might consider exploring, including Reiki, Matrix Energetics, Qigong, or shamanic healing. Another excellent option is to further develop and access your psychic abilities to find a well-suited technique for the given situation. The more that you do this, the easier it will become.

I also encourage you to check my websites (curtremington.com) and (meditationresources.net) for new books and articles on healing.

While performing a healing,
the appropriate technique will come to me,
through intuition or through my spirit guides.
~Mary Remington, clairvoyant energy healer.

CHAPTER 8
GETTING ANSWERS

In the process of learning life's lessons, we all have questions that we would love to have answered. *What are my key lessons for this life? How can I get along better with my spouse? Why is my boss so difficult? Is that guy I met really as nice as he seems? Is the new job I applied for a good fit for me? What is blocking me from accomplishing all that I want to? Where did I leave my car keys?* You can probably think of many more.

Knowledge Comes from Knowing

"Knowledge comes from knowing," is very wise advice that Chief, my Sioux spirit guide, gave to my wife during a reading she did for me. We sometimes do readings for each other.

What does that mean? she wondered. When she relayed the information to me, I knew immediately what Chief meant. "Knowing" referred to psychic intuition. In other words, by reaching a calm, meditative state, posing a question, and letting the answer come back to you, you're tapping into a higher source that's beyond your conscious mind. This is how Siddhartha Gautama (Buddha) arrived at many of the teachings that Buddhism is based on. In fact, many spiritual leaders have gained great wisdom this way. It may not make you a great spiritual leader, but by tapping into your own intuition you can acquire some important information.

At first, it may seem like a very subtle difference between psychic intuition and consciously thinking of an answer. So how do you tell the difference? The lack of effort is a big clue. If you let go of your thoughts, and something comes back to you as words or as an idea, then it probably is your "knowing" or psychic intuition. Another sign that it came from a psychic source is a response that you didn't expect or hadn't thought of, but that makes sense or sounds like a logical choice.

Where does psychic information come from? One of the most important sources is your "higher self." If it isn't completely clear yet what your "higher self" is, you're not alone. It is a concept that I may not fully be able to define until I reach the spirit world. In the meantime, you can think of it as your subconscious, your soul, or your spiritual self. It is eternal, wise, and more spiritually enlightened than your ego or conscious mind.

Communicating and aligning with your higher self can give you a sense of well-being and make your life more fulfilling and successful. It can also provide you with answers to life's important questions. The idea for this book, and much of what's in it, came from my higher self.

Connecting with Your Higher Self

It is easier to access your intuition after you've run your energies and reached a light meditative trance; however, it is possible to get information anytime. Just quiet your mind, hold the intention of using your intuition, and ask a question. Tune into the first response that you get. Try not to second-guess it. The response may be an idea that seemed to appear without you consciously creating it. Intuition may at first feel like our own thoughts, but with practice, you can learn to tell the difference. If the first thought to pop into your head is unethical or a bad idea, then you should question the source. It could be your own wishes, or it could be one of those trouble-making spirits. True intuition usually makes perfect sense but may seem like something you wouldn't have thought of. The thoughts that follow that first impression are probably your own rational mind processing the information.

Example

On the way home from a friend's house, Karla realized she'd been preoccupied and did not recognize where she was. Arriving at a T in the road, she had no idea which way to turn. Instead of guessing, she pulled over to the side of the road and accessed her intuition. Immediately, she got a response: *turn left.* She had been thinking about turning right. Three blocks after turning left, Karla reached a major road that she recognized.

Another Example

Dave had a long list of work that he needed to get done, but he never seemed to have enough time to do it. He realized that meditating was worth his time and could even help him work more efficiently. Sitting down to meditate, Dave ran his energies, then tuned into the eight jobs on his list. By the time he finished meditating, he had a logical order and understood the reason to do them in that order. He also realized that when he had been trying to think of a logical order, his dislike of cleaning had been clouding his judgment.

Information from Spirit Guides

Your guides and angels signed up for the job of helping and protecting you as you make your way through life on earth. Undoubtedly, they have been there many times for you, without making their presence known. You may have had a sense of danger in the road ahead, or you suddenly got an inspirational idea. It is very likely that your spirit guide or guardian angel was speaking to your subconscious. By purposefully communicating with them, you can gain another great source of information or help. They're happy to oblige.

Contacting Spirit Guides

By following these exercises, you can take the first steps to intentionally communicating with your guides. Start with grounding and running your energies. Once you're in a calm, meditative state, with your eyes closed, send out a thought requesting contact with a guide. With your thoughts, say "hello," followed by whatever other introduction seems appropriate.

Although you may not see them, they will get your message. They can see and hear you, so ask or say whatever you would like. They are very understanding and are glad to be acknowledged. Let them know what you want help with or what you would like to know. Looking for a response, pay attention to any images or thoughts that come to you. The guides can communicate in a variety of ways, sending images, thoughts, or feelings. You may get only a sense of knowing what they meant, or they may actually communicate in your preferred language. Be aware that spirits can have a sense of humor and may kid around with you, so don't take everything too seriously. The more you run your energies and practice this, the better your communication and understanding will become.

Example

Daphne meditated and held the intention to contact a spirit guide. An image started to take shape of a tall, thin rabbit, which seemed to ask, "What's up, Doc?" Daphne is quite serious, so she sure didn't expect Bugs Bunny as a spirit guide. She sensed her guide's purpose was to remind her to have more fun in life and to laugh once in a while.

Another Example

Once she was in a meditative state, Rhonda requested contact with a spirit guide. A woman in a long robe appeared. Rhonda felt a strong maternal love from this spirit. She also sensed that part of the guide's purpose was to help with Rhonda's developing interest in spirituality.

Working with Your Guides

Developing a closer relationship with your spirit guides is a great experience. They provide comfort, protection, healing energy, and help with difficult decisions. I feel that they deserve a great deal of gratitude. Now that I'm more aware of them, I thank my guides regularly. They undoubtedly appreciate it.

While writing this book, I called on spirit guides often for help. In fact, before starting the book, I communicated with Chief. He had suggested writing the book but told me the idea actually came from my higher self. Chief was just passing the message along to my conscious mind. I felt hesitant about writing it, not believing that I knew enough to write an entire book on meditation. Chief assured me that my higher self knew a great deal about meditation, and that I just needed to get started on writing. He also reminded me about a life we had together as Buddhist monks. I started asking specific questions, such as how long should the book be? Looking for a page count, I was told to write enough to cover the subject and not worry so much about details. He did add that one hundred or so pages should do but that making it clear was much more important than how long it should be. After all, it was to be called *Simple Meditation.*

What about including color photos, since I love my pictures? Nope, he said, you need to keep the cost down. These were very helpful and specific suggestions, which are typical of the kind of information Mary and I receive. When you first start communicating, the information you get may be somewhat less specific in nature, but it will still be helpful. Communication varies from person to person. Maybe you'll get very specific details, such as how to assemble an intergalactic teleporter out of garage-sale electronics, or you may get a general idea, such as that your son could use a lot of support at this time in his life.

Working with Roses

The rose has been an important symbol throughout history. The ancient Greeks and Romans identified it with their goddesses Aphrodite and Venus. To Christians, it symbolized the Virgin Mary. Roses have also symbolized the wounds of Christ or his resurrection. To a florist, they have many meanings, depending on the color. A red rose symbolizes love; white, purity and innocence; pink, appreciation; and yellow, friendship.

Many psychics use the image of a rose in a variety of ways, including a method for releasing energy during meditation.

Releasing Energy with a Rose

If you're trying to relax, but frustration from the day is making it difficult, imagine the energy from your frustration going into a rose visualized in front of you. You might see the energy as a dark, smoky substance. Once you feel the energy is there, destroy the rose by exploding it or make it disappear with a pop. By visualizing the rose, you are actually creating one on some level. When you destroy it, what you're doing is neutralizing the energy, not hurting anything. Creating and destroying roses can be a meditation by itself, as it releases and neutralizes energy. It also gives you practice in visualization. You can use this technique for releasing all sorts of negative energy.

Rose Reading Exercise

You can also use roses to "read" a question. Let the reply come back in the characteristics of a rose you visualize in front of you. Either ask the question and then create the rose, or create a plain white rose and see how the rose changes when you ask the question. If there is a person involved in the question, the rose could represent that person. For example, you might ask, "Is that guy I met really as nice as he seems?" See what kind of rose you get. Perhaps the rose will wither, which can tell you something about the relationship. If the question is about two people, use two roses and see how they relate. Is one taller (more dominant) than the other? Do they lean toward or away from each other? If you're considering two possible destinations for your vacation, try looking at a rose for each. Which one looks better?

Roses come in many colors, and each color can have its own meanings. Red may indicate anger, passion, or another strong emotion. Pink often indicates caring or female energy. Blue can represent calm or healing. Green can indicate growth or change. Yellow can indicate strength or wisdom. Purple is a powerful color and can indicate leadership or spiritual transformation. Color may even have a particular meaning for the person viewing the rose. Intuition is helpful here. Roses also come with closed blossoms, partially open or in full bloom, possibly indicating the level of growth if it's symbolizing a person. Stems can be weak and crooked, strong and straight, or anything in between. Many leaves on the stem may indicate a lot of creative expression. Many thorns may indicate a prickly person or situation.

The more roses you read, the more familiar your own symbolism will become. For me, white roses can indicate spiritual purity or protection, but I've also found they may indicate someone in nursing or another medical profession. It must be the white uniforms. Maybe for you, blue will indicate something about water or pink will indicate love. There isn't one set of rules for symbolism. It can be different for each person.

Examples of Rose Readings

Putting this into action, let's say you just met your sister's new boyfriend, Dirk, at a family get-together. He is outgoing, but you have a strange feeling about him. Out of concern, you decide that you will do a rose reading on their relationship. After going through your initial steps, you create a rose for your sister and another for Dirk. Looking at his rose, you notice that it's tall and straight, but it has some black spots on the closed blue blossom.

Your intuition tells you the spots respresent shady aspects of his character, while the closed blossom indicates he has growing up yet to do. The stem has many thorns, which seem to indicate a bad temper. As you look at her short rose, you notice that it leans toward Dirk's. The stem seems weak. The yellow bud is also fairly closed, and parts of the petals seem to be getting sucked off and pulled toward Dirk's rose, as if he's draining her energy.

I think you were right in having a strange feeling about Dirk. Now that you have this information, you need to decide what to do with it. Demanding that your sister leave Dirk may not be the best course of action. People aren't always receptive to information that goes against their thinking, and there is the issue of others being on their own path with lessons to learn. If it were me, I'd delicately point out that Dirk may not be the best choice of boyfriends.

Your psychic intuition will help you get a sense of what the rose's features indicate. Trust your intuition on this. As you practice this, you may develop more and more of your own symbols, which is excellent as long as you can understand them. One of mine is gray spots. Whenever I find them on a rose, they seem to indicate that the person is stuck on some issue related to the question being asked.

For a more positive example of a rose reading, let's say you've been contemplating signing up for a yoga class, and you wonder if this is a worthwhile idea. First, you create a rose for your present self. A yellow rose appears with a weak stem and many thorns. Next, you pose the question and watch the rose as the stem strengthens and straightens while many of the thorns disappear. You also note that the blossom starts to open and the color shifts toward green, indicating change and growth. It looks like a fantastic idea.

Clairvoyant Images

As you meditate more and work with visualizations, different clairvoyant images and symbols may come to you. Sometimes they're literal; for instance, seeing a desk may indicate schooling or an office job. A house could be your home, or it might be symbolic, representing a feeling of security. An image of an anchor could indicate someone who loves boating, or it could be symbolic of something that ties you down or gives you stability. Interpreting symbols is easiest by accessing your intuition while viewing your clairvoyant images.

Oracle Cards

Oracle cards can be a quick and amazingly accurate method for getting insight into a question or situation. The decks are similar to Tarot cards, but they tend to be simpler and less likely to have dark or negative images. Each oracle deck is based on a theme, like angels, totem animals, or fairies. Doreen Virtue[10] has decks that come with very helpful booklets; however, there are many good decks available from a variety of sources.

Validation Comes with Experience

When first using these techniques, it's natural to wonder whether you're getting this information psychically or unconsciously making it up. I overcame this doubt by performing many psychic readings. Often, I would see an image or get a message that meant next to nothing to me, yet the readee would know exactly what it meant and how it pertained to their lives. I soon became confident that the information was real and that I was getting it for a reason. An example of this was a reading in which the symbols I saw included a doorway, champagne glasses, an unusual round object, and a gathering of people. When I finished the reading, the readee told me she

10   Doreen Virtue is a fourth-generation metaphysician that works with the angelic and elemental realms. http://www.angeltherapy.com/.

was throwing a surprise birthday party for her husband. The doorway represented bringing people into her home, while the glasses and people represented the party. The description of the round object fit a wall ornament she was making him for his birthday.

During another reading, an outgoing and rather pushy spirit named Bob interrupted me. He just wanted to say hello and make some small talk. I asked the readee if she knew of such a person. She told me that she sure did. He was the sociable neighbor across the street who had died a couple of years ago.

My wife and I now use these techniques daily, gaining insight from our guides or higher selves. In addition to getting help in writing this book, we have better information for decisions. We gain insight into why people behave the way they do. We help others with their issues, and we stay in better contact with friends and family, whether they are of the physical world or the spirit world.

All great men are gifted with intuition.
They know without reasoning or analysis,
what they need to know.
~Alexis Carrel (1874-1944),
French surgeon and biologist.

CHAPTER 9
WALKABOUT OR VISION QUEST

Now you know how to meditate, connect with nature, contact a spirit guide, and get answers to important questions. How do you put these tools together to find your direction or purpose in life? You could do what spiritual seekers have done for thousands of years: venture into the wilderness on a vision quest or walkabout. These seekers include spiritual leaders such as Jesus, Buddha, Mohammed, and Moses, along with Indigenous Australians, Native Americans, and countless other people throughout history.

The word *walkabout* is often associated with Australian Aborigines, who would break away from their usual routine to venture into the outback on a spiritual quest, sometimes for six months or more. Maybe this was Forrest Gump's real motivation when he decided to "go for a run." I don't know about you, but even the word *walkabout* has strong appeal for me. Along with what you could learn, there is the adventure, freedom, and escape from routine.

Like the Aborigines' walkabouts, Native Americans had a similar rite of passage—the vision quest. They would venture into the wilderness in order to meet their totem animal and find direction in life. This was a shorter quest, three days or so, typically without food and with less wandering. They would spend most of their time in one place, often sitting in the middle of a circle of rocks, waiting on their vision.

Although not as common now, people (including some Aborigines and Native Amercians) do still set out in the wilderness on spiritual quests, some without even knowing what they are looking for. As for walkabouts, each year a few hundred through-hikers cover one of the major long-distance trails such as the Appalachian, which is 2,175 miles in length, or the Continental Divide Trail, which covers 3,100 miles. The Pacific Crest Trail, which runs near my home base, is 2,650 miles long. Surely it would take a strong incentive like a spiritual quest to get someone to walk so far.

A walkabout experience can consist of a much shorter trip. Maybe your walkabout doesn't even have to be a walking experience. In much of the world, a canoe, raft, or kayak trip may be a better way to find seclusion, like many of my trips growing up in Minnesota or my more recent Idaho raft trips. For those of you who aren't up to roughing it, you may even accomplish all that you want by setting out in your car, RV, or boat. Getting away for a quest experience can be a great adventure, no matter how you get there, as long as you spend time in nature contemplating, meditating, and making a spiritual connection.

There are organizations that specialize in vision quest experiences, or that make it part of their program such as Outward Bound and School of Lost Borders. Rachel, one of my teenaged daughters, crossed the Olympic Mountains on a three-week backpacking trip with Rite of Passage Journeys. Her two-day solo vigil on a beach in Olympic National Park was the most memorable and life-changing part of her trip. The following year, she signed up for a two-week trip in the North Cascades with the same organization.

Some people's experience is about facing fears and gaining confidence. For others, it may be an intensely spiritual experience, motivating them to reexamine themselves and decide on a new direction in life. Now that you're armed with new meditation skills, a quest would be a great opportunity to practice these. You may even find that your direction is fine and that you just need a new way of looking at life. As Marcel Proust, the French novelist, said, "The real voyage of discovery consists not in seeing new landscapes, but in having new eyes."

My own spiritual experiences, both in nature and in doing clairvoyant readings, have motivated me to change my course. As my psychic abilities developed, my viewpoint changed. I came to fully grasp that we are eternal souls with a temporary body. Viewing life that way changed my priorities. Helping others became more important to me, while acquiring money and material possessions became less important.

Worries and problems seemed less significant when I looked at them in the big, eternal picture. Figuring out what is important on my spiritual path became more of a focal point.

On a vision quest or walkabout you may receive powerful suggestions from your spirit guides, totem animals, or your higher self regarding positive ways to change your life, such as:

- Pursue a career that you enjoy
- Express your creativity through interests such as music, art, dance, or writing
- Let go of fears
- Meditate
- Have fun and enjoy life
- Help others. Relationships are what we're here for
- Forgive others, and let go of grudges
- Love is the answer. *To what?* Everything!

For many of us, life has become too routine: work, eat, TV, then sleep, followed by more of the same the next day. A walkabout or vision quest is a great first step to breaking out of that. Maybe your life isn't routine, but has been deeply shaken by a traumatic event, or maybe you're a teen, going through all the enormous life changes that age brings about. These are all examples of ideal times to embark on a walkabout or vision quest and examine your life, redefine goals, and develop a deeper spiritual connection.

Through meditation, you can prepare for a walkabout. While meditating myself, the following exercise came to me. Like a walkabout, this visualization takes you on an adventure into nature.

Inspirational Venturing Out Exercise

As you're seated comfortably, take a deep breath and close your eyes. Relax each part of your body, working down your neck, shoulders, back, and all the way to your feet. Once you're fully relaxed, imagine getting up and stepping onto a white sand beach. The sea is aqua-blue and gentle waves are lapping at the shoreline. As you step forward, visualize soothing bright light from the sun and sky soaking in, especially through the top of your head. This healing light causes the denser energy of your troubles and cares to flake off and fall away. Soon all that's left is the shape of your body, made of light. With each step you become lighter and more filled with energy, able to run and jump effortlessly on the beach and feel the soothing power and purity of this place.

If you want, dive into the water and swim, enjoying its cooler healing effects. After swimming as long as you'd like, walk back out onto the beach to a marble bench. Sit down and watch a golden sunset as you dry in the sun. Once you're ready, walk back across the beach, feeling lighter and healthier than you did before.

Embarking on a Walkabout

To embark on a walkabout, you don't have to be a great spiritual leader, live near the Australian Outback, or leave for six months. You can do what I did—decide on your goals and improvise. What's important is that you get out into nature, have a greater purpose, and are flexible. You may have a life-changing experience.

Throughout my life, I've been drawn to secluded outdoor experiences in the mountains, forest, or even my nearby neighborhood woods. Part of the draw might be my subconscious past-life memories of ventures into the wilderness, along with my childhood memories. When I was three or four, our Oregon backyard adjoined a creek and woods. I persuaded my parents to leave me out in the yard for a night with only a sleeping bag. In the middle of the night, it began to rain. Not only did I sleep through the rain, but I also slept through being carried into the house by my worried mother.

Later in my childhood, and into my teens, I'd camp alone in the Minnesota woods or on the islands of the St Croix River, spending hours or days practicing survival skills, communing with nature, and reading Tarzan or science fiction books.

These trips could have been even more powerful had I known the meditation techniques that I know now. Instead of spending so much time reading Tarzan books, I might have been having meaningful conversations with my spirit guides or deeply connecting with the quantum universe. My wife and I now meditate on almost every trip we make into the mountains or out to the islands. It's heavenly to connect with remote and beautiful places like the secluded beaches in Washington state's San Juan Islands or an alpine meadow in the North Cascades.

My Own Quest Experiences

To put my theories to test, I set out into the wilderness, like spiritual seekers before me. Unfortunately,

I'm one of those who couldn't afford six months in Australia, or even three weeks in the Olympic Mountains. I settled on a few days of backpacking in North Cascades National Park, Washington, a two-hour drive from home. The trip was a wonderful experience, and I accomplished a lot. Still, I felt there was more to do, including journaling more experiences to write about in this book. A month later, I took a three-day boat trip into the San Juan Islands, which are also conveniently close to my home. If you don't accomplish everything in the first trip, you may also decide on multiple trips, especially after you find what a wonderful experience it is.

For the North Cascades trip, time suddenly become available so I threw gear together the night before and left mid-morning for the park. For your own walkabout, I recommend planning well in advance, packing what you need, eliminating what you don't need, and making a list of your goals.

Once I got to the park and left my car behind, I didn't encounter another person all the way in. My route started in lush rainforest and climbed steadily to jagged snow-covered peaks near Cascade Pass. The mountains had received twenty inches of new snow in the prior few days, causing a few complications including wet feet. (This is not unusual for mid-May in the North Cascades.) High in the valley, I decided to camp in front of a large stone outhouse, the only patch of dry ground I could find. Spectacular views surrounded me, including Cascade Pass, Cascade Peak, Johannesburg Mountain and the valley from which I had just climbed.

When I decided on a second trip to the San Juan Islands, I debated loading my gear into a kayak and paddling to a quiet beach on Cypress Island. Upon further reflection, I concluded that with my Mirage 232 powerboat, I could get there faster, plug my laptop into the boat's battery, and get more writing done. With the meditation techniques you now know, I believe you can be flexible and don't necessarily have to rough it. If health holds you back from a bigger adventure, you can use these techniques at your local park or in your own backyard.

Instead of a rugged backpacking trip, on my second, more *flexible* vision quest, I decided to bring plenty of food, my laptop and to sleep in the boat. I needed to test my theory, that you can use these techniques without really roughing it. I couldn't see much sense in depriving myself of food or sleep, when I was perfectly capable of accomplishing my goals and contacting my totem animal and spirit guides with a full stomach. The truth is, you might get a stronger sense of satisfaction if you do rough it a bit.

With my gear loaded, I set out for Cypress Island during a small-craft advisory, driving into pounding seas for most of the twenty miles. The winds were 15 to 25 knots, so it wasn't terrible, just a tad on the rough side. At a place called Viti Rocks, strong tidal currents created powerful rapids with standing waves, whirlpools, and water converging from many directions. If I had gone by kayak, the wind and tidal currents would have been quite hazardous. Luckily for me, the conditions were no problem for my boat.

The surging water and waves provided a brief thrill, then I continued on to Cypress, tied to a moorage buoy, and arranged my gear for sleeping in the boat. The island is one of the least developed in the San Juans, with approximately forty residents and 5,500 acres, most of which is evergreen forest. That night, the wind occasionally howled and swung the boat in an arc around the buoy, while small waves caused just enough rocking to be soothing.

During my second day at Cypress, I hiked eight miles without encountering another person. Instead, I found a network of trails, small lakes, and an old airstrip recently planted with seedlings. During the hike, I worked at staying in the present, tuning into my surroundings, and writing down thoughts or messages that came to me.

My Wife's Quest

After three months of hearing about quests, and my wonderful experiences, my wife decided to do her own vision quest. She picked a remote riverfront site in a national forest campground near Mt. Baker,

Washington. She enjoyed her quest so much that she felt nostalgic about leaving the circle of rocks near her campsite by the river. On her drive home, she felt elated, like Moses coming down from the mountain.

What Makes a Walkabout Special?

A backpacking trip or any other trip into nature can be a delightful adventure. By adding a few more steps and putting your new meditation techniques into practice, the trip could be a life-changing experience. These steps might include:

- Connecting with nature
- Facing and overcoming fears
- Paying attention to your dreams
- Reviewing your life
- Examining relationships
- Making spiritual connections
- Examining your life's direction and purpose

Following these steps is what sets a walkabout apart from other trips. If health or time prevents you from doing any kind of trip, you can accomplish these steps at home. An environment with peace and quiet is all you need. As author Lillian Smith said, "No journey carries one far, unless as it extends into the world around, it goes an equal distance into the world within."[11]

As you do these things, keeping a journal of your experiences gives you an opportunity to go back and review what you've learned. Some of your thoughts or experiences may not even seem that significant at the time; instead, their deeper meaning is revealed later.

11 Lillian Smith, American writer (1897–1966).

Finding Your Path Meditation

Once you're situated comfortably, start by grounding and running your energies. Then visualize yourself walking on a path. You can pick the terrain. It might be woods or a meadow, along a beach or in a jungle. Soon, you come to an intersection. Visualize one with three choices in front of you. Do you keep going straight, take the trail to the left, or take the one to the right? Make a choice and take that trail. Follow it for a while, taking note of what's around you. Keep going until you go over a hill or around a curve. Where did that path take you? Are there any buildings? Do you see people or animals? Was the path straight or curved? Was it high, low, or flat? How does this place relate to where you came from? These images may be symbolic of what is going on in your life. Use your intuition. What is it telling you?

Example/Pyramid Visualization

Lucy visualized a lush jungle with birds singing and a light breeze rustling the leaves. She made her way down the path and came to an intersection in the trail. Her intuition told her to take the path to the right. The trail became darker and more quiet as the trees became thicker. She kept walking, feeling a twinge of apprehension. The trail started to climb, and she imagined each step as she made her way up the path. Then the jungle opened into a large clearing with an ancient pyramid. Lucy followed the path to the pyramid, then made her way up a set of steps. Reaching the top, she felt powerful energy rising from within the pyramid. At the same time, energy seemed to be emanating from the heavens. Lucy felt that the path represented her own spiritual quest, and the pyramid symbolized a powerful connection with the earth and the spiritual realm.

For one of your meditations, you might consider following the same path Lucy took and experience the energy of this ancient pyramid.

Really Connect with Nature

Nature is created beautifully and perfectly by God and advanced spirits. Wherever you go, nature holds wonderful details that can capture your attention, as long as you take the time to look and listen.

In the North Cascades, I watched the changing sky as the sun dropped behind the ridge, and I listened to the occasional rumble of an avalanche on the mountains across from me. Other sounds I tuned into throughout the day included a small distant waterfall, the wind blowing through the trees, and an almost constant whoop, whoop, whoop from the woods above me, which I eventually determined was the mating call of a blue grouse. The beauty of the jagged peaks around me almost constantly commanded my attention.

In the San Juan Islands, the sound of the waves lapping at the boat was almost hypnotic. A curious harbor seal swam by, stopping to watch me from a distance. Near shore, a great blue heron stared intently into the water, waiting for little shiner perch to jump.

Overcome Fears

Before embarking on a walkabout or vision quest, you may have to overcome some fears before venturing out. For many, just the thought of spending a night alone in the woods, or of intentionally contacting spirits can be intimidating. My wife and I backpack and camp regularly, but the thought of camping alone caused her a fair amount of apprehension. People who challenge themselves by facing their fears usually arise from the situation with a newfound confidence. Mary certainly did.

But it's equally important to have respect for the wilderness. and you are strongly encouraged to take every necessary safety precaution. Even on short day hikes in the mountains, I carry the "ten essentials" to survival, as recommended by the Mountaineers.[12] I also closely check weather and avalanche reports to gauge the risk, and I pack whatever gear I may need to make it home. If you're new to wilderness adventures, consider using an organization or plan a trip that's well within your capabilities.

As for a fear of spirits, remember that you are a powerful and eternal spirit yourself, and you have loving protectors like your totem animal, spirit guides, and guardian angels. I've heard firsthand from a number of people that actually encountering a protective spirit or a sign from the spirit world

12 http://www.mountaineersbooks.org/client/client_pages/Media%20Archives/mtn_
media_TenEssentials.cfm.

has ended their fears. As a child, my friend feared the supernatural, until one day an angel entered her room. She felt so much love and protection that she was no longer afraid.

Many people go through life afraid of change or of trying new things. If that's you, and you're thinking about a vision quest, that's a big step in the right direction. There are many more places, hobbies, people to meet, and adventures out there. Write some ideas down and vow to try them. Why not experience as much as you can in this life?

You may have other fears to examine and face during a quest, such as a fear of health issues or death, financial problems, or any of countless possibilities. While on your quest, look at what fears you have. How have these fears affected you? Have they held you back from doing all that you want to do? If you face them, what is the worst-case scenario that could happen? Sometimes, it's losing a job or ending a relationship. Depending on the situation, this often turns out to be a blessing, making room for something new in your life.

Mary looked at her fear of shifting careers into work that focused on energy healing and spirituality. She meditated on this and got encouraging messages. "Let go of perfect pictures. Believe your needs will be met. Tap into your past lives as a healer." And, "This is your God-given gift." With these inspirational messages, she let go of much of her fear.

A vision quest group leader I interviewed told me of his own quest experience. He had recurring dreams of snakes, which seemed to symbolize his fear of major changes that were taking place in his life. One of the final days of his quest, he sat on a cliff overlooking the Columbia River, contemplating his life and sensing the presence of spirits around him. As he made his way back to camp, he came face to face with a rattlesnake, which faced him with its head lifted. He stopped and watched the snake, and a sense of calm suddenly overcame him. Not only was he not afraid of the snake, but his other fears, symbolized in his snake dreams, were gone too.

Dreams

While on a walkabout or quest, important messages may come to you through your dreams, such as the example with snakes. To remember your dreams, make remembering your intention before going to bed, then wake slowly, replay your dream immediately, and write it down. Through dreams, I've received many important messages from the spiritual realm, including some from my spirit guides and deceased loved ones. Often, they were quite literal, or I've known what the symbolism meant. If you don't know immediately, try meditating on it, and the meaning may come to you intuitively. During my quests, my dreams were often symbolic, so I had to do a meditation to make sense of them.

In the North Cascades, I had a strange dream about waking up in a house with an anxious client just outside my bedroom door, looking for his real estate appraisal. After he left, I looked in the bathroom mirror and found myself wearing a dark wig and fake eyebrows. The symbolism seemed to

indicate that writing appraisals is not my real purpose in life. It has, however, been helpful for paying
the bills.

In the San Juan Islands, I dreamed of a mouse
that I chased and struggled to catch, as it kept making
a mess and causing more turmoil. Once I finally had
my fingers around it, I wasn't sure what to do with it,
so I let it go. This mouse seemed to represent my teenaged daughter. She too has caused a fair amount of
turmoil over the past couple of years, while we worried
about her safety, her future, and struggled to bring her
under control. She's now eighteen, and the dream was
indicating that at some point soon, we'll have to give
up trying to control her, let go, and hope for the best.

Life Review

In doing a life review, you can work at consciously
remembering as much as possible about your life,
or you can meditate and see what comes up. As I
did that, I saw myself walking in the woods with
my grandfather as a child, reminding me of my lifelong love for forests.

While sitting in the mountains, it seemed natural
that my early love for wild places would surface in a
meditation, but I believe it also came up because this
was a key theme in my life. My love for the outdoors
is one of the main motivators for my decisions and
behavior. Another strong motivator was my desire,
from an early age, to find my soul mate. Now that I'm
familiar with many of my past lives, I think I was
aware at some level, that connecting with my wife,
Mary, was part of my destiny. We've been married to

each other in many lifetimes, dating back thousands of years. We've also played other important roles in each other's lives.

During the life review on her vision quest, she looked at her fear of change and how she's overcome much of that in recent years. She also looked at her key personality traits such as her compassion, work ethic, sensitivity, and occasional stubbornness. She looked at each of these traits and how each has fit into and affected her life.

For you, something completely different may come up. What are your priorities? Your traits? Is there a significant theme? Have you been satisfied with the course of your life? Your relationships? Your job? What would you want to change?

Direction in Life

After reviewing your life, you may conclude there are things you'd like to change. Perhaps that job is just something that pays the bills, but not a career you ever enjoyed doing. Have you neglected hobbies or friends because of a lack of time? Has fear or hesitation stood in the way of getting to where you'd like to be? Where would you like your life to be a year from now? Five years? Ten years? What steps could you take to get there?

A quest or walkabout is an ideal time to look at and make changes in the course of your life. If we just keep stumbling along without direction and goals, we're not likely to get to where we want to go. This is such an important subject that I'll explore it more deeply in the next chapter.

I looked at my twenty-year career as a real estate appraiser. It had provided financial security and a strong income for most of those years. However, it had also provided plenty of stress and had never truly felt like a career fit for me. For one thing, creativity is not appreciated. If it had not been for my concerns about security and fear of failure, I might instead have pursued freelance writing years ago.

Examining Relationships

In looking at relationships, the obvious one I wanted to change was with one of my teenaged daughters. She has been a challenging case of teenage rebellion and apparently thinks that we're overly strict parents. At times, I've wondered if perhaps we are. I meditated on the situation and psychically looked into her heart. What I saw deeply moved me. She loves her parents much more than she ever lets on. I also saw that she would benefit from more quality time with each of us. At the same time, she puts as much distance between us as she can and doesn't realize how much we love her.

On Mary's quest, she looked at some early relationships in which she'd been hurt. She examined how that caused her to be reluctant about connecting with others. She also looked at what she learned from those relationships and forgave the people who had wronged her. After that, she looked at key people such as her parents, and children, examining how she could help each of them on their current paths.

Who have been the significant people in your life? What did you learn from them? Do you have relationships that also need work? If so, try looking at life from that person's point of view. What's motivating them to do what they do? What events and relationships molded them? How could you improve the situation? Although I still don't agree with my daughter's perspective, meditating gives me a much better understanding of why she does what she does.

Spiritual Experience

Seeking a vision or spiritual connection is a compelling reason for striking out on a quest. It's what inspired countless young natives to venture out and meet their totem or power animals. As a trained clairvoyant, I seek and experience such visions regularly, and I've found that people do indeed have totem animals, along with other spirit guides and guardian angels.

First conscious contact with your guides can be an incredibly moving experience. One day at home,

before I started clairvoyant training, I tried a meditation to contact my spirit guides. A sparkling light entered the room and flew around. I felt the presence of a loving spirit, and then I closed my eyes and saw a stream of images flashing before me, of people and places I don't remember ever seeing before. I felt in awe. The images eventually stopped, but the impact stayed with me. I wanted to know more about what is out there, and I wanted to communicate with my guides and guardian angels. Shortly after that, I signed up for my first clairvoyant class.

On my North Cascades quest, high in the mountains and close to heaven, I felt eager for another spiritual experience. Taking a deep breath of fresh air, I worked on a state of focused calm, closed my eyes, and called for my totem animal. A gray spirit wolf skidded to a stop in the snow in front of me. He let me know that he stays nearby, ready to protect me on the spiritual plane. He watches for dangers on the physical plane as well, sometimes sending a subtle warning of hazards ahead.

After the wolf faded, I called for another guide. Chief appeared, with long dark hair and buckskin pants. I asked him what else I should write about regarding this trip. He reminded me to focus on and describe more of the details of nature. I do tend to get caught up in my thoughts, which distracts me from staying in the moment.

Always appreciative of their help, I thanked them for all they do. My quest renewed my gratitude for my health, my family, my life, and for the fact that such a beautiful place exists only a two-hour drive from my house. Gratitude can help change your feelings to positive ones, attracting more positive things into your life. It's a high form of energy vibration.

When seeking your own vision, what you experience may consist of a sign in nature. A deer or bird that acts unusually may be trying to give you a message. Your dreams can hold messages, so pay close attention to them on your quest. While meditating, you can ask a question, quiet your thoughts, and see what comes. Often, a thought that pops into your mind may actually be a message from the spirit world rather than your own thought. This is how telepathy and intuition work. These messages may be accompanied by an image, like the spirit wolf I saw, or a strong sense of knowing the answer to your question. The more you practice this technique, the easier it becomes.

Mary first learned of her owl totem animal during clairvoyant training. The first night of her quest, she lay alone in her tent, feeling somewhat afraid. It took time, but as she was finally drifting off to sleep, she heard an owl calling from across the river. Soon, a second owl landed and joined in, closer to her tent, followed by a third and a fourth. All four chattered back and forth. In our many years of camping, we've never encountered such a thing. Mary knew the owls were communicating to her and trying to make a spiritual connection. She was so overwhelmed with joy that it brought her to tears. She felt very loved and protected and was no longer afraid. During the next day's hike, she came across a broken piece of a stump, in the shape of an owl.

The last day of her quest, Mary sat in her circle of stones by the river, contemplating her direction in life and asking for a sign. A short time later, a strange whirlwind of sand spun up from the mostly pebble beach. That seemed a clear sign to investigate, so she got up and walked over to where the sand-spout had been. She found a small patch of sand with several footprints. Soon, she realized that most of them had only the heel print remaining. She quickly made the connection between "heel" and "heal." She felt a clear message that healing had always been her passion and was the path that she should follow.

Reviewing What You've Learned

During my hike down from Cascade Pass, I placed each step carefully, trying to avoid breaking through the hard frozen snow. As I made my way, I reflected on and reviewed what I had learned during my meditations.

For some people, their vision quest is such an intense experience that coming back to the normality of civilization is a real adjustment. If so, give yourself time. You may need to rest or to contemplate how what you've learned will fit into your life. You may decide that there are changes to be made regarding your career, relationships, or other aspects of your life.

I spent the rest of my weekend in the mountains gathering my thoughts and scribbling notes in a pad. On the way out of the park, I stopped at a massive tree and contemplated its history, which extends back a very long time. I wondered how many others might have passed by it on their own vision quests.

Final Thoughts

A walkabout or vision quest can be an inspirational, potentially life-changing experience. You can undertake one without compromising your safety or pushing yourself beyond your physical limits. Rather than depriving yourself of comforts, it's more important that you get this on your schedule, that you make time for yourself alone in nature, and that you follow the exercises in this chapter or in a similar format.

If you'd prefer to leave trip planning to someone else, a variety of organizations that specialize in vision quest trips are out there to help. The best one for you would depend on your individual circumstances and location. If you'd rather plan your own trip, Denise Linn has an information-packed book called *Quest: A Guide for Creating Your Own Vision Quest*.[13] Please visit my websites (curtremington. com) and (meditationresources.net) for information on the *Walkabout Workbook* (Fall, 2011), with more details on the steps to prepare for your quest along with pages you can fill in to record insights and the highlights of your experience.

---

13 Denise Linn, *Quest: A Guide for Creating Your Own Vision Quest* (New York, NY: Ballantine Publishing Group, 1997). www.deniselinn.com.

Twenty years from now you will be more disappointed by the things you didn't do than by the ones you did do. So throw off the bowlines, sail away from the safe harbor. Catch the trade winds in your sails. Explore. Dream. Discover.

~Mark Twain (1835-1910), author and humorist.

Chapter 10
Transform Your Life

Although we're on the last chapter, we're not even close to being finished. Spiritual growth is a long, ongoing process. Why do you think we reincarnate so many times? You can have a lot of fun along the way. Reading this book has been an important first step in your spiritual growth, but an even more important step will be to follow through and use the meditation techniques covered here.

Meditation is a skill that you learn by doing. It gets easier with practice. I hope you've been practicing these techniques as you made your way through the book. If not, please start today. A good goal is to meditate for at least twenty minutes every day and possibly longer on days that you're doing reading or healing work.

When life gets hectic, or some major trauma occurs and throws you off track, you may feel there isn't enough time to do everything. It's at times like these that meditating is most important and can get you through these periods of growth. It can help you remain calm and grounded, so you can handle your problems rather than letting them get the best of you or put you in a state of panicked, overwhelmed stress. Meditating is always worth the time. If you do get off schedule, just start back up and make it a daily habit again.

Which Meditations to Use

For your daily meditation, grounding and running your energies are the most important and are a logical way to start any other meditation. Grounding will help you reach a calm and secure state. It will also give you a place to release anything you want to let go of. You might even want to check your grounding throughout the day. Running your energies flushes out the blocks to your emotional, physical, and spiritual well being.

On a given day, your current circumstances may determine which technique to use next. If someone in your life is in need of help, you could consider doing some energy healing. If you need insight into an important issue, you could use a technique for getting answers. If you'd just like to relax and enjoy yourself, do a fun visualization exercise. And if you just can't decide what to do, scan the table of contents and tap into your intuition. It's very likely the meditation that is just right will pop into mind.

Our Life Purpose

With all this meditating, you will connect and communicate better with your higher self and with the spiritual realm. In the spirit world, advanced spirits experience what I would truly call heaven. They live in a place of incredible beauty, with crystal cathedrals, castles, vast forests, canyons, mountains, and stunning colors that we don't experience on earth. They have the freedom and ability to create and heal with energy. They have access to infinite knowledge and incredible psychic abilities. They have friendship, camaraderie, and absolute love.

When in heaven, we are motivated to learn all we can and to advance our spiritual development by increasing our capacity to love, help and understand one another. This might be because it's the right thing to do—it's innate. As a part of God (or the Source or whatever you choose to call it), we want to become more like God.

When we inhabit a body here on earth, we don't always remember that *our life's purpose* is to further our spiritual advancement in the ways described above. Many of us get off track for a lifetime, or even numerous lifetimes. That's okay. We have eternity, and we're increasing our knowledge during those lifetimes, even if we're only making minute spiritual progress.

Individual Lessons

Along our path, we have individual, deeply personal lessons for each particular life. In early lives, people are just learning how to survive. As we advance, our lessons tend to become more specific. For me, big lessons in this life have included letting go of anger and judgment. For someone else it may be letting go of guilt or learning how to work hard. Others may be experiencing what it's like to be poor or rich, or they may need to learn how to put their own needs aside to take care of someone else.

Not only do we have our own lessons to work on, but an important part of our purpose is to help others with their lessons. Before you were born, you may have chosen or agreed to your role as a child, parent, sibling, or spouse.

All these lessons are enough to keep a person busy for many lifetimes, but I believe your life purpose can still hold more. In the *Seven Spiritual Laws of Success*, Deepak Chopra[14] states that everyone has a unique gift or special talent to give to others, something that makes the giver happy when they're doing it. Is there something you could do that would bring you great joy? What are your skills and talents? Maybe there's a career or hobby that's called to you, but you've avoided, preferring to stay in your comfort zone. You might find a very satisfying volunteer job. If nothing fits this description at first, try out different things. Discover what you enjoy. For insight, meditate and connect with your higher self and your spirit guides. They undoubtedly know what brings you great joy.

For more information on our spiritual path and life

14   Deepak Chopra, *Seven Spiritual Laws of Success (San Rafael, CA: Amber-Allen Publishing, 1994), 100*–101. www.chopra.com.

purpose, the Michael Teachings (michaelteachings. com) provide some fascinating material, like descriptions of the spiritual roles, soul ages, and personality traits. You might also try Michael Newton's *Destiny of Souls: New Case Studies of Life Between Lives* (Llewellyn Publications, 2001), which describes our time in heaven between lives. For information about your own personal spiritual path or past lives, consider visiting a clairvoyant or a hypnotherapist who does past-life regression or life-between-lives work.

Once you have some ideas regarding your life purpose, you can start taking steps and making choices that put it in motion. This puts you in control and can be very empowering. For instance, you may decide that an important lesson in this life is overcoming fears. Maybe you'll decide to start that new business, go back to school, or take up that new sport. The following visualization meditation is an exercise for working toward your life purpose.

Transform Your Life Meditation

Imagine that you're on a snow-covered mountain, mindfully placing one foot in front of the other as you climb steadily upward. Use trekking poles, if you like, visualizing each pole plant and each step. The snow crunches as you place each foot. You may encounter a ridge of snow or other obstacle, but you make your way over and keep climbing for as long as it feels right. As you climb, feel yourself becoming lighter and stronger. Feel the cold, clean air as it enters your lungs. Your confidence grows in your ability to accomplish what you want.

As you reach the top and stop climbing, look out at the valley below. What do you see? Enjoy the moment! Feel the energy of the heavens above and the earth below. Sense your connection to them and to all that is around you.

Finding My Purpose in Life

Until I started meditation and clairvoyant training, I hadn't given a lot of thought to my purpose in life. If I had to put it into words, I might have said something such as "work hard, get what you want, and retire happy." That may be pretty close to a life purpose for many of us. Once in a while, however, a nagging thought haunted the back corners of my mind, telling me there was more to it than that.

Now that I view myself as an eternal spirit, my perspective is much different. Discovering my past lives made it easier to make sense of what I'm working on now. I've realized that I'm quite a slow learner, at least in regards to spiritual lessons. My first life dated back many thousands of years. With so many lives under my belt, it seemed that I should be doing something very spiritually advanced such as feeding the poor or discovering the cure to cancer. Instead, I had spent much of my life writing real estate appraisals, and I was still a bit temperamental and selfish. After I began meditating, my initial reaction had been to question, "How could I be so spiritually slow?"

Having looked a little deeper, I have some insight into this. My goal-oriented warrior nature probably held me back, since spiritually enlightened values such as love, forgiveness, and helping others aren't high on a warrior's priorities. Also, like many of us, I would forget what I'm here to learn, and I would hone whatever skills were necessary for that life. I became skilled at fighting, farming, running small businesses, inventing, and more.

During my more judgmental years, I believed that everyone could be financially successful if they would just work harder. It worked for me. I've since learned that it wasn't just hard work, but many lifetimes' worth of practice that played a role in my success. Among less financially successful people, there are also plenty of old souls that don't set monetary success as a priority. They've already experienced that in prior lifetimes and would rather work on relationships or helping others.

If I'd understood any of this, I wouldn't have been so quick to judge other people as lazy. Instead, I might have judged myself as shallow. Now, along with not judging others so harshly, I've decided to not judge myself so harshly either. I may be a slow learner and have no doubt endured lots of karma for my warrior ways, but I've also experienced and learned an awful lot about life on earth over the course of lives. Learning slowly and thoroughly isn't all bad.

More recently, I've received strong messages that I need to change some of my warrior ways. As a Native American, I became chief and worked to promote peace. It was not that I was against battle, but because I saw the futility in continuing a fight that couldn't be won. It may be that I was put in that position so I could learn that lesson. Instead of fighting, I worked on Native American rights and education.

After that life, I was a Jewish teen in New York during World War II. Lying about my age, I enrolled in the army and was killed on Omaha Beach during the Normandy Invasion. Fighting didn't work out well for me in that life either.

In my current life, I have three daughters, who respond much better to love and understanding. Again, I'm reminded that fighting is not always the answer. I've learned how to be respectful, to listen, and to try to understand the other person's point of view. The bravest choice is to stand up for yourself—without hostility. Aggression and anger seem only to reflect more hostility back to you.

I eventually realized that there are also benefits to my warrior nature. I've been willing to take on challenges and to continue working hard, accomplishing where others might have quit. Warriors are also very physical, staying active and enjoying life on this physical planet. This may also be part of the reason I've been reincarnating so long. After much introspection, I've become more accepting that I am what I am and that there are pluses and minuses to my nature, as there undoubtedly are to yours too. I've also realized that everyone is different, and each person has his or her own strengths and weaknesses. It makes more sense to appreciate and accept that, rather than to judge them for being different.

I have come to learn my purpose in this life, and it is taking me in a new direction. I'm helping friends and family whenever I can, writing this book, creating websites, speaking and sharing what I've learned with you. It is my hope that this will help both of us on our spiritual paths.

Final Thoughts

Meditating will help transform your life in many positive ways. It will connect you with your wise higher self, the spirit world, this beautiful planet, and those around you. Imagine having access to such a gift. And through this gift you may learn a few things about yourself that you may not have known. You've had many lifetimes before this and done a variety of fascinating things. You do have psychic abilities. Through meditation, you can begin to feel more relaxed, content, and happy. Meditation will help you transform your life and will help you to realize that you are a unique and beautiful soul.

Man is not a being who stands still, he is a being in the process of becoming. The more he enables himself to become, the more he fulfills his true mission.
~Rudolph Steiner, Austrian philospher
and founder of Anthroposophy

Bibliography

Angelo, Jack. *Hands-On Healing: A Practical Guide to Channeling Your Healing Energies.* Rochester, VT: Healing Arts Press, 1994.

Assorted authors. *The Holy Bible: English Standard Version.* Wheaton, IL: Crossway Bibles, 2003.

Belhayes, Iris. *Spirit Guides.* San Diego, CA: ACS Publications, 1985.

Bourgault, Luc. *The American Indian Secrets of Crystal Healing.* Cippenham, England: Quantum, 1997.

Braden, Gregg. *Fractal Time: The Secret of 2012 and a New World Age.* Carlsbad, CA: Hay House, Inc., 2009.

———. *The Divine Matrix: Bridging Time, Space, Miracles and Belief.* Carlsbad, CA: Hay House, Inc., 2007.

Brainy Quote website. http://www.brainyquote.com/.

Brinkley, Dannion. *Saved by the Light: The True Story of a Man Who Died Twice.* New York, NY: Harper Collins Publishers, 1994.

———. *At Peace in the Light.* New York, NY: Harper Collins Publishers, Inc., 1995.

Brown, Sylvia. *Life on the Other Side.* New York, NY: Penguin Group, 2000.

Buhlman, William. *Adventures Beyond the Body: How to Experience Out of Body Travel.* San Francisco: HarperSanFrancisco, 1996.

———. *The Secret of the Soul.* New York, NY: HarperCollins, 2001.

Cayce, Edgar. *Reincarnation & Karma.* Virginia

Beach, VA: A.R.E. Press, 2006.

Chestney, Kim. *The Psychic Workshop: A Complete Program for Fulfilling Your Spiritual Potential.* Avon, MA: Adams Media, 2004.

Chopra, Deepak. *The Seven Spiritual Laws of Success: A Practical Guide to the Fulfillment of Your Dreams.* San Rafael, CA: Amber-Allen Publishing, 1994.

Choquette, Sonia. *Your Heart's Desire: Instructions for Creating the Life You Really Want.* New York, NY: Three Rivers Press, 1997.

———. *Ask Your Guides: Connecting to Your Divine Support System.* Carlsbad, CA: Hay House, Inc., 2006.

Dalai Lama, His Holiness the. *The Art of Happiness.* New York, NY: Riverhead Books, 1998.

Davich, Victor N. *The Best Guide to Meditation.* New York, NY: Renaissance Media, Inc., 1998.

Dyer, Wayne W. *Change Your Thoughts – Change Your Life: Living the Wisdom of the Tao.* Carlsbad, CA: Hay House, Inc., 2007.

———. *Excuses Begone: How to Change Lifelong, Self-Defeating Thinking Habits.* Carlsbad, CA: Hay House, Inc., 2009.

Fanning, Patrick. *Visualization for Change.* Oakland, CA: New Harbinger Publications, Inc., 1988.

Fermilab. US Department of Energy. http://www.fnal.gov/.

Flora, Mary Ellen. *Chakras: Key to Spiritual Opening.* Everett, WA: CDM Publishing, 1999.

———. *Clairvoyance: Key to Spiritual Perspective.* Everett, WA: CDM Publications, 1992.

———. *Meditation: Key to Spiritual Awakening.*
Everett, WA: CDM Publications, Inc., 1991.

Foster, Steven. *Vision Quest: Personal Transformation in the Wilderness.* New York, NY: Fireside, 1992.

Gauding, Madonna. *The Meditation Bible.* New York, NY: Sterling Publishing Co. Inc., 2005.

Hall, Judy. *Crystal Healing.* London: Godsfield Press, 2005.

Harner, Michael. *The Way of the Shaman.* New York, NY: Harper & Row, 1990.

Hay, Louise L. *You Can Heal Your Life.* Carlsbad, CA: Hay House, Inc., 1999.

Hicks, Esther & Jerry. *The Law of Attraction: The Basics of the Teachings of Abraham.* Carlsbad, CA: Hay House, Inc., 2006.

How to Meditate website. Guided Meditation Techniques. 2010. http://www.how-to-meditate. org/.

Katz, Debra Lynne. *You Are Psychic.* St. Paul, MN: Llewellyn Worldwide, 2005.

———. *Extraordinary Psychic.* St. Paul, MN: Llewellyn Worldwide, 2008.

———. *Freeing the Genie Within: Manifesting Abundance, Creativity & Success in Your Life.* Woodbury, MN: Llewellyn Publications, 2009.

Lawrence, Richard. *Unlock Your Psychic Powers.* New York, NY: St. Martin's Press, 1993.

Linn, Denise. *Quest: A Guide for Creating Your Own Vision Quest.* New York, NY: Ballantine Publishing Group, 1997.

MayoClinic.com – "Meditation" article. http:// www.mayoclinic.com/health/meditation/HQ01070.

Meadows, Kenneth. *Shamanic Experience: A Practical Guide to Psychic Powers.* Rochester, VT: Bear & Company, 2003.

Meditation Center website. http://www.meditationcenter.com/.

Meditation Resources website. http://meditationresources.net/.

Michael Teachings website. http://www.michaelteachings.com/.

Miller, Jill website. http://www.jillmillerpsychic.com/.

Moody, Raymond, Jr. *Life After Life.* St. Simons Island, GA: Mockingbird Books, 1975.

Moondance, Wolf. *Vision Quest: Native American Magical Healing.* New York, NY: Sterling Publishing Co., Inc., 2004.

Myss, Caroline. *Anatomy of the Spirit.* New York, NY: Harmony Press, 1996.

Newton, Michael. *Memories of the Afterlife: Life Between Lives Stories of Personal Transformation.* Woodbury, MN: Llewellyn Publications, 2009.

——. *Life Between Lives; Hypnotherapy for Spiritual Regression.* St. Paul, MN: Llewellyn Publications, 2005.

——. *Journey of Souls: Case Studies of Life Between Lives.* St. Paul, MN: Llewellyn Worldwide, 1994.

Plotkin, Bill. *Soulcraft: Crossing into the Mysteries of Nature and Psyche.* Novato, CA: New World Library, 2003.

Pope, Joya. *The World According to Michael: An Old Soul's Guide to the Universe.* Fayetteville,

Index

A

B

C

D

N

O

P

Q

About the Author

Curt Remington has meditated regularly since childhood. Those early meditations involved venturing into the woods and tuning into the beauty of nature, listening to the wind in the trees, or just sitting quietly and taking in the energy of a scenic place.

Since that time, Curt has learned and developed many more meditation techniques and exercises such as those for healing with quantum energy, improving relationships, and accessing psychic abilities.

Curt received his first formal meditation training as part of an advanced clairvoyant program, where he learned techniques for accessing and working with the vast field of quantum energy that makes up our universe.

Curt's education includes a bachelor's degree in Business Management, classes and workshops on a variety of subjects, and reading hundreds of non-fiction books in an endless quest to expand his knowledge.

For more information, please visit http://curtremington.com and http://meditationresources.net. Both sites contain a variety of meditations, spiritual articles, and Curt's nature photography.

9 781936 610068